Curling Basics

A comprehensive guide to the game of curling

edited by

Roy Sinclair

WS
Publishers

First published 1998
by
WS Publishers
The Studio
Old Ballikinrain
Balfron by Glasgow
G63 0LL Scotland

A CIP catalogue record for this book
is available from the British Library

ISBN 0-9532115-1-7

RCCC Rules
Reproduced with their permission

Cover produced by
Optical Creative Imaging
Glasgow

Typesetting by FRED

Printed in Great Britain
by
Antony Rowe Limited
Chippenham

This book is dedicated to all curlers.

In the spirit of curling it has been a team effort,
with special thanks to the contributors:

Derek Blyth
Irene Hird
Judy Mackenzie
Roy Sinclair
Jack van der Spuy

Illustrations by Celia Norman Smith

As in curling, there is no intended discrimination between the sexes. To simplify explanations throughout this book the male gender has been used as neutral, with no disrespect to the female gender.

Contents

Introduction

The sound of a curling stone roaring down the ice, especially on the rough surface of a frozen pond, can seem frightening to the beginner, and in a full ice rink the noise can at times be truly deafening. No wonder that it is called "the roaring game", yet there is no aggression, no real animosity, no serious argument. There is fun, determination, concentration, frustration, sometimes jubilation.

Curling, as we know it today, evolved from common pastimes into something of a ritual and from there to a regular game. Though many countries might want to claim the credit of its origin no-one can say for certain, because most of those who played this kind of game 500 years ago couldn't write, and therefore recorded history is no proof.

There can be no doubt that people, young and old, played on frozen ponds or lakes from Iceland to the Low Countries and even the high Alps. There is recorded evidence of games, but not of the origins of curling as ancient as those, and historians will debate the finer details for many years to come. Not many of these games have survived, yet people still play on the ice for much the same reasons as they did then.

There is an Alpine game called *eisschiessen* ("ice shooting"), played then and still played today – a player with his *eisstock* tries to lie closest to a wooden block when he slides it down the ice, perhaps displacing another stick, or the block. Last stick holds the advantage, as in curling. Then there is quoits, also still played today, and the game of coiting, or kuting. Quoits was played in the fourteenth century and banned by Edward III, who fortunately didn't ban coiting as well. Coiting is the game Scots played on frozen ponds with stones called loofies, and this name for the game of curling was still used in the 19th century in Ayrshire. Coiting was curling, though perhaps not as we know it now.

There is no evidence to suggest that curling did *not* originate in Scotland. Imagine a black frost setting in, a real hard one that freezes the surface of a pond solid and safe. The people are huddled together in their small houses struggling to keep warm before a hungry fire, and after a day or two the smoke wins and they are driven out into the fresh air. What can they do? Play on the ice.

In those days of the 16th and 17th centuries the winters in Scotland were extremely cold and ice very common. There was little or no drainage and the fields were littered with frozen ponds; there was nothing better to do but keep busy and keep warm, and nothing warms a body quicker than sweeping the frost before a curling stone. Living in houses without windows and negligible heating from smoky fuels was not fun, but curling against a challenging neighbour in the fresh country air certainly was. And the neighbours it had to be, because there were no real roads and travel beyond a certain distance was a waste of time and something few could afford.

The game of curling evolved along with the improving roads and railways, faster communication with the new penny post and better organisation. In the beginning competition was *with* your neighbour *against* the weather; soon it became *with* the weather *against* your opposition. A great many things change over a period of several centuries, and curling changed with them. Fairness became an issue, and before long the stones were becoming standardised. Rules were introduced, from a simple do or don't to a sacred obligation never to touch a running stone. Before long groups formed into simple clubs to curl against neighbouring clubs, and everyone waited for some courageous individual to bring the whole game together.

The man who gave to curling its consolidation was John Cairnie, but he was not alone. He provided his character, energy and no doubt some of his money to build on the work of many others and founded the Grand Caledonian Curling Club, at a meeting in Edinburgh in 1838. When a new railway line enabled Queen Victoria, age twenty-three, to make her first journey to Scotland with Prince Albert a few years later, she was given a demonstration of the game on the ballroom floor at Scone Palace, in Perthshire. It must have ruined the fine floor but it made the point, and before long Prince Albert agreed to become the game's first patron. The Grand Club soon became the Royal Caledonian Curling Club, which it still is.

Meanwhile many Scots were emigrating to Canada. The Canadian winters were, and still can be, as severe as the Scottish winters of the 16th century, and it didn't take much to establish the game of curling. Soon there would be ten curlers in Canada for every one in Scotland, and it is still by far the largest curling nation. Distances however were vast and travelling 50 miles through deep snow took time, and very soon small, makeshift buildings were erected to serve as meeting places or shelters. The rink would be prepared outdoors and those not curling – or snowed off the rink – would socialise within, and when the snow proved too much of a hindrance the rinks themselves were covered by many an ingenious method. When stones were in short supply they sawed blocks off logs, and the straw brooms widely used for cleaning houses proved ideal for cleaning snow and frost off the ice.

Wherever the game was played, there was always a strong element of brotherhood. This was due to the social advantages within a cold climate as much as to the rural spirit of a hard battle against nature, and the majority of curlers are still from farming communities. The RCCC strove to promote this policy of brotherhood as much as the organisation of the game itself, and to this day curling is outstanding amongst all modern sports for its fraternity and goodwill. It was a gentleman's game when the farmers played on their frozen ponds and when landowners played in the new rinks in the cities, and is a gentleman's game still – as well as a lady's, and that of a young lad or lass.

Yet it is so much more, because it is truly and totally also a team game. There can be no other game, played by folk from six to sixty-six and beyond, in which each member of its team of four is equal, with equal responsibility to play his stone to perfection and equal duty to sweep another's stone to perfection. There is never a dull moment (unless you're losing badly and want to go home!), and when the four members of a team curl as a team no opposition can be comfortable. In a long and hard winter, with morale as low as the daylight hours, there can be no game more suited than curling to lift the spirits of those who have to suffer the cold and damp.

Throughout its evolution the game of curling has been wisely guided to become a supreme pastime in winter. Curl but once a week and the winters become friendly and healthy, and while spring brings relief from too much curling autumn can't come soon enough to take to the ice again. Now that curling has evolved into a true winter sport and an official sport on the Olympic agenda, no sport can be better suited to express the Olympic ideal: it is not to win, but to take part – and enjoy.

There are many different ways in which new curlers are attracted to the game. Often a friend will bring someone along to have a go, or the school might try to recruit a few new curlers, or a local authority offers curling as one of its sports through an over-fifties' or women's society, or television had a good programme on and you want to have a go. It doesn't matter which, as long as you accept the opportunity. You will be welcomed and helped in every way because curlers are like that and one day, not too long ago, someone did it for them.

It is the purpose of this book to help new curlers learn about the game and enable them to take part. Beginners will soon evolve into competitive curlers and some into serious Olympians, and there will be many coaches along the way to help them with their problems. For someone totally new to curling the advice is to read this book carefully, then go and have a try. Read it again afterwards to answer new questions and return to it whenever in doubt. Before long you'll be drawing the button with comfort, though it isn't easy, and only practice can make perfect.

The Game

The game of curling, they say, is like bowls on ice, where players with their bowls/stones play to end nearest the target. This is true but there the similarity ends, because curling is much more than that. At the very least the aim is to slide a stone down a sheet of ice and have it stop as near as possible to the button, but the aim of the game is that the opposition must be unable to do anything about it.

Suddenly, from a very simple concept, curling is raised to a game of great skill, strategy, finesse, exertion, endeavour and – above all – comradeship. A team of four players who regularly curl together become a unit of one with tremendous faith in each other, and they will play as hard as they can to make their eight stones count. But clearly it is extremely difficult and even unlikely for a team to score eight shots in a single end, so the aim is and must be to score at least one. And if the opposition holds the best stone with only one stone to play, the skip who plays that last stone must either rearrange what there is or better it, which can seem impossible but is often achieved. As any committed curler will profess: nothing is impossible, and never say die.

A Team consists of four Players, except in Pairs (two) and Points (one). Each player has two Stones to play, alternating with the opposition stone by stone. A coin is tossed between the Leads and the winner decides which team plays first, and he usually puts in the loser to retain the advantage of that last stone. The Lead plays a stone first, followed by the opposing Lead, then their second stones; the Seconds follow, then the Thirds and finally the Skips. They play sixteen stones and the End is complete, the Score is decided and the House is cleared. The winning team of the end is obliged to go first on the next end, the scores accumulate and after ten ends, or when the Bell rings, the Game is complete.

During the game the skip in charge stands in the house directing play, with the other skip outside the house awaiting developments. He holds his Brush in one hand and indicates with the other – the player aims at his brush and applies Curl by turning his playing hand towards the side indicated. This simply means that the player applies clockwise rotation to the stone if the indicating arm is on the player's left, and anti-clockwise rotation if the indicating arm is on the player's right. Watch from behind a player and notice how the stone Draws away from the indicating arm and the Line of the brush, often as much as six foot by the time it reaches the house, and notice especially how little rotation is applied to the stone for it to draw. One rotation down the length of the ice is sufficient and two or three on the safe side, but give it a spin and it won't draw at all because its own centrifugal momentum will keep it out. It is after all a heavy curling stone and not a flying saucer.

With the skip and one player occupied, the other two members are having a rest. Not so. They follow the played stone down the ice and Sweep in front of it, then they don't, then they do. These Sweepers are amazing, some running along or doing sideways skips like children in the gym, others sliding smoothly on one foot while propelling themselves with the other; some Sweeping nowhere near the stone, others concentrating on the square foot in front of and so close to the stone that they risk touching it. What they're trying to do is complex and not easily grasped. They could be cleaning the ice, or helping the stone to travel farther than it would have done otherwise, or prevent it from drawing, or all three. For now it is best to settle for the knowledge that they are sweeping.

Look at the skip, he's excited. His face is turning an ever deeper red as he shouts. He bounces up and down in his encouragement (legal) and slaps the ice with his free hand (not strictly legal) and bangs his brush on the ice (illegal). The sweepers' faces turn red too as they furiously sweep the ice, placing more and more weight on their brushes as the stone's momentum dies away. The player takes off after the stone to help, even the skip leaves the house to come and help. The stone crosses the Hog Line and approaches the house, and suddenly they stop sweeping as if someone had given a command. The stone comes to rest and they turn away breathless but smiling, the sweeping had worked.

The skip is in charge and gives the command. He decides what to do or what not to do and makes his wishes known with obscure gestures, yet everyone seems to understand. Abandon the warmth of the galleries for a few minutes to go down to the side of the ice and listen to the noise they make, and it can be deafening. Hear the comments and observations they shout at each other, communicating in single words or short sentences, strange words with little meaning that somehow get the messages across. There's no time for long sentences, the commands and replies have to be instant and the players' reactions must be instant. It's called teamwork, such as no other game can generate.

Watching a game in progress it soon becomes obvious that no two stones are played quite the same. The skip might be holding his brush in the same place, but while some can play the line required others are more erratic. Some stones need sweeping and others don't, some need a lot of sweeping and others only a little. Some stones travel at a terrific speed while others seem barely to be moving. It becomes apparent that a stone which doesn't reach the hog line is removed from play, as is a stone which crosses the Back Line, or those crossing the Side Line and not drawing back into the playing area. The area of play is defined: between the side lines, from the Hack where a player places his foot for grip to the back line behind the house at the far end. But beware, it isn't quite that simple.

Study the diagram on page 39 for a while. Down the middle of the sheet is the Centre Line, from one end to the other. Across the sheet there's a Foot Line and the hack, then a back line, a Tee Line, a hog line, a long space, another hog line, a tee line and a back line, and the foot line and hack at the other end. The hack has two halves, each with a foothold – right-handed players must play from the left and left handed players from the right, so that the stone starts its travel down the same centre line. From the hack to the first tee line a player can change his mind when playing his stone, because as long as the stone doesn't reach (touch) the line he can go back to the hack and play it again. This doesn't happen very often, but is worth knowing.

Next comes the hog line and a player must, definitely must, release – and be clearly seen to release – the stone before it reaches the hog line. If the stone touches the line with even a finger still in contact it is an illegal stone and must be removed from play. The released stone becomes a Running Stone which, if touched by a player, or his brush, or the pen that fell out of his pocket, becomes a Burned Stone and must be removed from play. Once a stone is released, and it may only be released once, no-one or nothing is allowed to touch it, because it will alter its line and usually this will be unfair. Curling is a fair game.

The stone travels down the ice and reaches the further hog line. If it comes to rest before it crosses the line it is dead, useless and in the way, and must be removed. It must cross that line and not be touching it to remain in play. However, if it hits another stone which has crossed the line but doesn't cross the line itself, then it is in play, because if the other stone hadn't been in its way it would probably have crossed the line. If it comes to rest after the hog line but before the house then it is in the Free Guard Zone, which will receive attention later. If it reaches the house it is potentially scoring a shot, but of course the opposition is going to do something about that if they can. If it passes through the house and crosses the back line it is out of play again and is removed, but if it is still touching the back line it is in play.

As for the side lines which divide the sheets of ice, it is worth noting that a stone is allowed to touch or even cross the side line, but it must not touch anything and must draw back into the area of play to remain in play. If it comes to rest touching the outer circle while also touching the side line it does remain in play. However, if it touches the Side Board or a dividing board and bounces back like a clever bit of billiards it is out of play, because a stone is not allowed to touch the side boards.

The sweeping areas too are defined, as in the diagram on page 40. Between the two tee lines anyone can sweep a stone, provided it is a running stone and belongs to your team. Once it reaches the tee line in the house only the skips can sweep, and both skips can sweep with equal right. If a skip has played the stone in question, leaving his third in charge of the house, then only the third may sweep behind the tee line, along with either the opposing skip or the opposing third. It is not allowed for anyone to sweep a stone that is not moving, as it is not allowed for skips to sweep behind the tee line before the stone reaches it. If someone could find a suitable penalty it would be made illegal in the rules, until then it simply isn't done.

Another important point concerning the sweeping is that only one brush per player can be used, which he chooses before the game and is not allowed to change unless he breaks it or it becomes unusable, and then he must choose a similar brush. On the other hand players of the same team are allowed to swap brushes between them.

Touched running stones are burned and must be removed. There are complicated exceptions which could need an umpire to make a decision, but it is always the duty of the player(s) who touches the stone to own up immediately, for the stone to be removed without further ado. If the opposition touches your running stone it could, or could not, have been on purpose, and if the skips can't sort it out with big smiles it won't be a very good game of curling. The rules deal with this. A much more common problem is when someone moves a stationary stone which isn't running at all, but is lying in the house minding its own business. Again the skips have to sort it out, and more often than not they do so by simply putting the stone back where it was. If it is more complicated, as when a stone is kicked out of the way to make room for another, there is clearly a need to enforce the rules to the letter. The rules deal with this too. Over and above all these problems it remains the duty of all players to do their very best not to touch stones, because it can become very complicated and often unsavoury.

The art of the perfect stone does exist. First consider the requirements, which are quite simple: line, and length. A stone which is exactly on line and played with perfect weight will usually stop where you want it to stop, but not always. The variables accumulate quickly when you add a few sweepers, the odd scrap of dirt or hair on the ice that stones invariably find, changing ice conditions during a game, or a run in the ice which the skip had forgotten to take into account. Suddenly the perfect stone seems impossible! It isn't, though, but some shots are easier than others and the most spectacular shots are often the easiest.

Consider the different shots. At the one end of the scale of weight is the lightest shot, a Guard Stone. It is played to reach the hog line but not the house, and if it doesn't reach the hog line is called a Hog and removed from play. If it reaches the house there's no real harm done but it's not a very good guard, and if it's out the back it can be considered a waste of everyone's time.

A recent development in curling has been to declare the area between the hog line and the house a Free Guard Zone (see page 122), meaning that the two lead stones from both teams may lie in this area and not be blasted from the rink by the lead players. Should the opposition lead hit your lead-guard stone *out of play*, accidentally or otherwise, it is returned and the offending stone is removed. Should they bump into it but not remove it from play there is no infringement of the rule and the stones remain where they finish. Once the seconds play their first stones the rule no longer applies. This development has changed the game for the better, forcing teams to play more of a drawing game and usually with more stones in the house. Remember however that a lead can, accidentally or otherwise, remove *his own* previous stone from play without infringing the Free Guard Zone rule.

A guard can therefore be an extremely important shot to play. On Keen ice, where a stone needs very little momentum to reach the hog line, it is a very difficult shot, but if it's what the skip wants it has to be played. The best policy is to play a little lighter than needed and let the sweepers work it in to where they want (don't do this too often or too badly or they won't be speaking to you, not because they don't like you but for want of breath!). Should you play it too hard and it stops in the house the opposition will almost certainly knock it out, and out the back is useless. If there is a shot in curling worth practising regularly it is the guard, especially to consistently stop a few feet short of the house. Line is less important than weight, particularly with lead stones, but when a third or skip wishes to guard a stone in the house they will make sure that both line and weight are as near perfect as possible – a guard that doesn't guard its subject is useless too.

Also, a guard just short of the house can always be Raised, or bumped up into the house, often ending behind the stone which had raised it and now guards it. Don't ever think a lead player is unimportant, he has the most difficult shot to master time and time again. The skip indicates that he wants a guard stone by holding his brush horizontally and/or tapping the ice in front of the house.

The next shot on the scale of weight is the Draw. It is only slightly heavier than a guard and usually has to either draw around a guard to lie behind it, or draw up to another stone in the house to lie tightly against it and so be very difficult to knock out. Both line and weight are important, and again it is wise to be a fraction on the light side and let the sweepers finish the job. It is the standard shot in curling by which all other shots are measured in weight, the shot most often needed to get out of trouble and most valuable if played well. Most skips have the experience to play it well and certainly should be able to, more often than not it is how the last stone of an end is played to either save the end or gain an extra shot.

Finer details of the draw include Front-house weight, where the stone stops before reaching the tee, and Back-house weight, where the stone crosses the tee, and stones played to either wing or side of the house. In all these it is only the line that differs, with the sweepers in control of distance. The skip will indicate a draw shot by simulating the intended line of the stone with his brush and then stopping where the stone should stop, often tapping the top of the brush with the palm of his free hand.

The next is Hack weight, in effect a heavy draw, which is used to bump a stone through the house but remain in the house itself. Because of its high chances of success it's a good percentage shot to play, but of course the opposition will be able to play the same shot if the stone is in sight. If it can be played with a slight angle on impact it will roll a little to one side and often finish behind a guard, which creates a problem for the opposition not so easily solved. A Hit-and-roll shot is not easy because both line and weight have to be judged continuously by skip and sweepers, and here experience and good sweeping quickly become evident.

The more common takeout stone is played a little heavier, at Barrier weight (also called Peel or Back weight), where the stone will be heavy enough to reach the back board or end of the rink. The faster a stone is played the less it will draw, so line becomes extremely important. At Strike weight, where a stone travels far and fast enough to bump into the back board with a considerable thump, there is very little draw at all, and if the stone is off the brush it will miss its target.

All takeout shots are played to remove stones from the house or from the guard zone, with very little emphasis on staying in play, and in the modern game these shots have resulted in empty houses with very low scoring. There is nothing wrong with adopting this seemingly aggressive kind of game which is in fact defensive, but it is boring to watch and boring to play and doesn't allow for the finer skills of curling to claim their rightful places. To sweep a stone hurtling down the ice at strike weight is difficult and dangerous, and beware of scattering stones into neighbouring rinks – they can ruin someone else's game if not his ankles. A skip indicates a takeout shot by touching the stone with his brush and then pointing his brush vaguely at the intended finishing point, and if he wants strike weight he will touch his shoulder. Also note that he isn't really allowed to tap the stone with his brush, for who can say he hasn't moved it, but skips do it all the same.

The "cannon ball", a stone thrown down the ice at such a speed that the impact with another claps light sharp thunder, is not a good idea. Some players insist on playing it, though, and once in a very long while it might actually be necessary, but the odds of it achieving an impossible escape from serious trouble are against you. Not only can it not be swept with any effect but it often moves so many stones that the opposition gains a shot out of it, and there's no success in that. Avoid it as best you can, if you break a curling stone through wilful bloody-minded play the manager will ask you to pay for it, and curling stones are very expensive.

It is obvious that there are always two players sweeping. This is not simply because they're cold and need to warm up, the sweeping is very important. On the one hand a well-swept stone will draw less, and on the other hand it will travel farther. If there is a guard and the stone is intended to draw around it and take shot, the shot would be virtually impossible without good sweeping – the skip and sweepers will control the line and weight and put the stone exactly where they want it, shaving dust off the guard but not actually touching it. To see it happen is a beautiful thing, and as close to a perfect stone as anyone could wish. The gallery will applaud.

Then there is the sweeping done by the skip behind the tee line, trying to sweep a very slow-moving opposition stone out of the house. All his weight is on the brush and he only uses his tip-toes for balance, and if he has the knack of good sweeping that stone will go out. Sometimes the opposing skip will even help him, though not out of sympathy, and that is a bonus, but only the two skips – or their deputising thirds – may sweep behind the tee.

Should a stone pass through the house and come to rest still touching the back line, it is of course still in play. If it is in the six-o'clock position the rules allow for a measurement to be made to see if it is in fact still in play, because the ice man might well have painted the line in the wrong place. An implement called the Six-foot Measure is used to measure from the tee line to the stone in question, and it will be either in or out. The same implement is used to decide if a stone is still in the Free Guard Zone, and not to be struck out, or is biting the outer circle and therefore a very legitimate target for the opposition – the measurement is made from the tee in the button and if the stone is further than six foot it is safe. Note that, once a stone has been measured and a decision reached, it may not be measured again unless it has been moved by another. No other measurements at the house are allowed until all sixteen stones have been played, and it is not a good idea to clear any stones from the house until the score has been decided. See also the note on page 38.

Turn the clock back a hundred years. Imagine a frozen pond, the temperature is minus fifteen and everything is frozen solid. A few locals have been watching the pond for days and decide the time has come: the ice is thick enough for curling. They scribe two circles, one with a radius of four foot and the other six foot. They measure the length and place a board or crampit on the ice for a hack; the ice is cleaned as best they can and the teams decided. Suitable stones are brought and they start curling; before long the onlookers gather, sustaining themselves with sips from their hip-flasks.

A dispute arises, so they mark out a hog line. The back line follows, then the side lines to keep the audience at bay. For the best part of two hours they play their game, stone after stone, sweeping and shouting, the audience cheering every good shot, deafening silence consoling the bad. The noise warms them all as it echoes through the frozen glen, and when the final draw reaches to take the shot, and the game, the roar of celebration can be heard for miles.

The modern game on a modern rink is no different in any respect, and if the audience is warmer in the gallery at least they're not in the way on the ice. The layout of the rink, the equipment, the rules and the spirit have all evolved into an organised, fair structure, yet they have changed very little. Curling has only become what it has always been: a game for all, with enjoyment for all. Whisky has not been mentioned.

Words

Curling words have evolved along with the game, and there are almost enough for a different language. This list is not exhaustive, as this is not a book about language, but the words listed here will come in useful sooner or later.

BACK LINE	The line behind the house. Once crossed, a stone is out of play (see Rink).
BACK-HOUSE WEIGHT	An indication of the momentum needed for a stone to reach the back half of the house, near the centre line.
BARRIER	Alternative term for the back boards.
BARRIER WEIGHT	An indication of the weight needed for a stone to reach the barrier.
BIASED ICE	Ice that isn't level, therefore stones fall out rather than draw.
BIG DRAW	When ice conditions cause the stone to draw more than usual.
BIG END	When a team scores three or more shots in an end.
BITER	A stone just touching the outer edge of the 6ft circle, potentially counting.
BLANK END	An end where no stone scores a shot.
BONSPIEL	A curling competition, or tournament, between teams at a chosen venue.

BROOM	A besom-type sweeping implement, with straw or synthetic bristles, mainly used in North America.
BRUSH	A brush-type sweeping implement, with hair or synthetic fibres, used for sweeping.
BURN	To touch a running stone; to remove a touched stone.
BURNED STONE	A running stone touched by a member of either team, or by their equipment.
BURY	To draw around a guard stone and lie hidden behind it.
BUTTON	The small centre of the circles.
CENTRE LINE	The line which runs down the middle from hack to hack (see Rink).
CHAP AND LIE	To remove an opponent's stone and stay in the house.
CLEAN	To sweep *lightly* before a stone.
CRAMPIT	A spiked metal footplate fitted to shoes for outdoor curling and now banned. A plate of metal or wood with spikes, now used as the hack in outdoor curling.
DOUBLE	A takeout shot that clears two opposing stones from the house.
DOUBLE ROLL-IN	To raise a stone to the house and roll in too.
DOUR ICE	Rough, soft, slow ice.

DRAW	The amount of curling movement to describe the distance from the direction of release to the intended target. A stone played to end in the house; an instruction to play such a stone.
DRAW WEIGHT	An indication of the momentum needed for a stone to end in the house.
DRUG ICE	Slow, difficult ice.
END	Component of a game, during which eight stones are played by each team in the same direction.
EXTRA END	The deciding end played when the score is level after all scheduled ends have been played.
FALL	A slope on the ice, causing bias and preventing expected draw.
FAST	A confusing word. See Heavy, Keen.
FAST ICE	Ice on which stones travel further under the same momentum, or less momentum is needed to reach a certain point.
FREE DRAW	To draw into an empty house, usually with skip stones.
FREEZE	A stone played with perfect weight to rest against another.
FRONT-HOUSE WEIGHT	An indication of the momentum needed for a stone to reach the front half of the house, near the centre line.

FROSTY ICE	Ice with frost on the surface, caused by high humudity.
GIVE ICE	To hold a brush for a player to aim at, as a skip to indicate the amount of ice needed to draw to a target.
GUARD	A stone played to protect another.
GUARD WEIGHT	An indication of the momentum needed for a stone to end in front of the house.
HACK	The block at each end of a sheet, usually of rubber, which provides the foothold from which stones are played (see Rink, page 39).
HACK WEIGHT	An indication of the momentum needed for a stone to reach the hack behind the house, specifically a light takeout weight.
HAMMER	Term used to indicate who has last stone.
HANDLE	Term to denote the rotation applied to a stone upon release.
HEAD	The house, the circles which a stone has to reach in order to count (see Rink). More specifically the house at any stage of play and the stones within.
HEAVY	A stone with too much momentum.
HEAVY ICE	Ice on which stones don't slide easily.
HIT AND STAY	To play a takeout which removes the target, and stay lying in place.

HIT AND ROLL	To play a takeout which removes the target, and roll to a different place.
HOG	A stone which fails to reach the hog line, and is removed from play.
HOG LINE	The line each played stone has to cross to remain in play (see Rink and Rules).
HOUSE	The circles which a stone has to reach in order to count (see Rink).
HOUSE WEIGHT	An indication of the momentum needed for a stone to reach the house.
HURRY	Instruction shouted for sweepers to sweep.
ICE	The distance given by the skip, between where the stone is aimed at (his brush) and where it should finish after curling. Call of alert to warn others when a stone might hit their feet (golf = fore).
IN-TURN	Slight rotation applied to a stone where the playing hand turns in towards the player (clockwise for right-handed players and vice versa).
IN-WICK	To glance off the inside of a stone and stop holding a good position.
KEEN ICE	Ice on which stones travel further under the same momentum, or less momentum is needed to reach a certain point.
KIPPER	Loose sole fitted to sliding foot as a gripper or anti-slide.

KUTING	An old term for curling, played with stones which had no handles fitted.
LAST STONE	Term used for the last stone of an end.
LEAD	Player who plays his two stones first.
LIE, LYING	To hold the shot nearest the tee.
LIGHT	A stone with too little momentum.
LONG GUARD	A guard stone far from the house.
LOSE ITS HANDLE	Term for a stone which loses its rotation usually because of dirt on the ice.
MEASURE	Term used for: The 6ft measure, to see if a stone is in the house or in play. Used during play, but see the note on page 38. The measure when an end is complete, to decide which of two (or three and more) stones is closest to the tee.
NO HANDLE	Term for a stone released without rotation, which curls little or erratically.
OFF THE BRUSH	Term for a stone not delivered at the skip's brush as required.
OUT-TURN	Slight rotation applied to a stone where the playing hand turns out from the player (anti-clockwise for right-handed players and vice versa).
OUT-WICK	To glance off the outside of a stone and move it closer to the tee.

PEBBLE	The frozen droplets of water applied to a sheet of ice before a game, reducing friction between the stone and the ice.
PEEL	A takeout shot where both played and struck stones roll out of play.
PEEL WEIGHT	An indication of the momentum needed for a stone to play a peel shot.
PICK UP	Term to indicate that a stone has caught something under it, causing it to deviate strongly from its direction of travel.
PORT	A space between two lying stones, large enough for another to pass through.
POT-LID	A stone lying on the tee or button.
QUICK!	Further encouragement from skip to sweepers to sweep even harder.
RAISE	To bump or move a lying stone a short distance further, usually into the house.
RAISE TAKEOUT	To strike a stone in front of the house and raise it to remove another from the house.
READING THE ICE	Anticipating how much a stone will curl, taking all the variables into account.
RINGS	The house.
RINK	The building where curling takes place. A curling team. The sheet of ice on which a game is played.

ROCK	North American word for a curling stone, seldom used in Scotland.
ROLL	The movement of a played stone after striking another.
RUB	A very slight contact between stones, sufficient to deviate the running stone a little from its course.
RUN	A slight worn hollow in the ice which makes it difficult for the stone to curl, often found beside the centre line where players' feet or stones slide.
SECOND	Player who plays his two stones second.
SECOND SHOT	The stone lying second closest to the tee (after the shot stone).
SHEET	The area where one specific game is played.
SHORT GUARD	A guard stone near the house.
SHOT	A played stone. The word used to indicate a point won at the end of a game
SHOT STONE	The stone nearest the tee during an end.
SKIP	Player who usually plays his two stones last, but not always. He is always the player who directs the game and decides strategy and ice.
SLIPPY SOLE	Loose sole fitted to sliding foot.

SLOW	A stone played lighter than asked for.
SLOW ICE	Ice on which stones travel less under the same momentum, or more momentum is needed to reach a certain point.
SLOW TAKEOUT	A takeout stone of sufficient momentum to reach the back board, slightly heavier than hack weight.
SPINNER	A stone which rotates too many times and therefore doesn't draw.
SPLIT-RAISE	A stone which raises another to count and rolls in to count as well.
SPLIT THE HOUSE	To have a stone lying to one side of the house and draw another to the other side to hold two "in the wings".
STEAL	To score shots in an end when you didn't have last stone.
STRAIGHT HANDLE	A stone released without applying rotation.
STRIKE	A shot which removes a stone or stones from the house.
STRIKE WEIGHT	An indication of the momentum needed for a takeout stone with more weight than the back board.
STRONG CURL ON THE ICE	When ice conditions cause the stone to draw more than usual.
SWEEP	Shouted by skip, for sweepers to sweep.

SWEEPING	Moving a brush or broom across the path of a moving stone.
SWINGING ICE	When ice conditions cause the stone to draw more than usual.
TAKEOUT	A shot which removes a stone or stones from the house.
TEE	The cross in the button.
TEE LINE	The line through the centre of the house at a right angle to the centre line.
THIRD	Player who plays his two stones third. Usually the vice-skip who stands in the house when the skip plays his stones.
TIGHT	A stone delivered with less ice than the skip indicated, nearer to the target than his brush.
UP!	Command by skip for sweepers to stop sweeping. He'll shout HURRY next.
WEIGHT	The momentum applied to a stone for distance.
WICK	A thin contact between played and lying stones.
WICK AND ROLL	To get a thin contact and roll away a little.
WIDE	A stone delivered with more ice than the skip indicated, wider from the target than his brush.

Scoring

The scores in curling are recorded on a board at one end of the rink as the game progresses. The process can seem complicated at first, but it's really quite straightforward.

For a stone to score a shot its nearest edge must be within the house, i.e. 1.83m (6ft) from the tee; all sixteen stones must have been played, and only the stones nearer to the tee than any stone of the oppsition score a shot each. As the painting of the outer circle, or the little hole drilled on the tee for measuring, is not always exact, it is often the case that a stone has to be measured with the six-foot measure to see if it does count. Also, when no clear decision can be reached between two stones a measure is called for, and an implement is provided by the ice rink for the purpose.

Who does what, and when. No stone can be measured until all sixteen stones of an end have been played, except with the six-foot measure to determine whether a stone is in the Free Guard Zone, or still in play at the back line (see note, page 38). Measuring in competitions is done by an umpire, often the manager of the ice rink, or someone deputised to do the job. Normally however the teams do it themselves, and it is considered the duty of the thirds to resolve the dispute and decide the overall score of each end. It is the duty of the second to record the score not only on the board but also the scorecard, although the third or skip often helps. A simple rule: if it's not your job, stay out of it, and that includes the house. It is important to record the score at each end, not only for the benefit of the players, but also for the audience all around the rink.

Two kinds of scoreboard are in common use. The North American board is found in many rinks in Scotland and is very simple, once you're used to it. The international board is more difficult only if you're used to the other and suddenly have to record a score. On both boards the details are recorded with little numbered disks of wood, metal or plastic, which hang from hooks at the appropriate end on the board.

Consider the North American board first. The blank board at the start of the game contains nothing except a row of numbers, which represents the score as it accumulates. The numbers of the ends are on the loose disks.

North American Scoreboard

Black												
SCORE	1	2	3	4	5	6	7	8	9	10	11	12
White												

In the first example Black loses to White by 6-8, with White coming from behind to win the game in the tenth end with a two. The second end was a blank end, where no stone scored, and the number hangs beside the board.

Black			1	5	7	9							
SCORE	1	2	3	4	5	6	7	8	9	10	11	12	
White	3		4		6	8		10					2

In the second example Black thrashes White by 16-3, and some care is needed to read the score. The ends were 1-B2, 2-B1, 3-W1, 4-B4, 5-B2, 6-W1, 7-B2, 8-W1, 9-B3, 10-B2.

Black	7	1	2	9		10	4		5			
SCORE	1	2	3	4	5	6	7	8	9	10	11	12
White	3	6	8									

The North American scoreboard is quick and easy to use, and requires less disks than the international board. Its only disadvantage appears when the score reaches double figures, but on the whole it remains the preferred board with most curlers who quickly grow used to it.

The international scoreboard probably became established because of its visual clarity, which can easily be duplicated on paper for official purposes. Here the ends are numbered on the board with the scores on disks, and the total is changed after every end.

International Scoreboard

		1	2	3	4	5	6	7	8	9	10		Total
Black													
White													

Again, in the first example Black loses to White by 6-8, with White coming from behind to win the game in the tenth end with a two. The second end was a blank end, where no stone scored, and is recorded by zeros, as are other spaces.

		1	2	3	4	5	6	7	8	9	10		Total
Black		3	0	0	0	1	0	1	0	1	0		6
White		0	0	1	2	0	2	0	1	0	2		8

In the second example Black thrashes White, who shakes hands after nine ends. Note how the unplayed tenth end is marked on the board.

		1	2	3	4	5	6	7	8	9	10		Total
Black		2	1	0	4	2	0	2	0	3	X		14
White		0	0	1	0	0	1	0	1	0	X		3

The international board has advantages, but many competitive curlers dislike it because it takes much longer to record a score with several disks to be found and hung in their places. Better learn to live with it, because it is the board used in serious competition and it's here to stay.

In most competitions and leagues a scorecard is used to transfer the scores to the official in charge. The details on these cards play an important role in the organisation of the game and should be filled in carefully, and signed by both skips after the game.

Scorecard

VENUE .... RINK ....
COMP .... DATE ....
TEAM 1 ....Black............ TEAM 2 .....White.........
Skip .... Skip ....
Third .... Third ....
Second .... Second ....
Lead .... Lead ....

2	2	**1**	0	0
1	3	**2**	0	0
0	3	**3**	1	1
4	7	**4**	0	1
2	9	**5**	0	1
0	9	**6**	1	2
2	11	**7**	0	2
0	11	**8**	1	3
3	14	**9**	0	3
2	16	**10**	0	3

Signed: Skip ....
Opposing skip ....

Note how the scores are entered with a running total of shots in the second column, and the ends are listed in the middle. With such a definite scoring system there is also no room for mistakes that might creep in, and the score is seldom queried.

In club curling the tradition is often to fill in the names of the players as first names only, which creates a friendlier atmosphere and also provides a means of learning someone's name without embarrassment. With the development of serious competition at national and international level the initials and surname have become the accepted entry. For anything other than club games it is important to use initials and surname, to enable secretaries to make important checks on information often months after the game.

Some might argue that no-one needs a scorecard. Not so, because they really are quite useful both during the game and afterwards. Most serious curlers will remember the score, end by end, for weeks afterwards, and the better the game the longer the memories. But many competitions continue throughout a season of curling, often culminating in a weekend of semi-finals and finals, and for these the scorecards are vital.

Although the scoring is accurate and very finite, the games are seldom so. Every game or competition will have its own rules of duration, some of eight ends or the bell and others ten ends or the bell. This simply means that, if the bell should ring while an end is still in play, another end cannot be played. But if the bell rings *after the last stone of the last end has come to rest*, another end can be played. Sometimes the bell doesn't ring at all because someone forgot, and this can easily result in the wrong team gaining an undeserved victory. Usually the skips will however agree to stop when the allotted two hours or so have passed.

The timing of sessions is important in the running of an ice rink. Staff need a few minutes to clean and/or pebble the ice before the following session, and there are curlers waiting to start their games on time if at all possible. If all games have to be of ten ends there will soon accumulate a delay of an hour, which causes total havoc. It is only fair and reasonable that all curlers do their best to play strictly to the rules in place and so contribute to the quality of the ice they play on.

Frequently a game may result in a draw, with both teams gaining equal shots in total. The easiest, and the norm, is to call it peels an go for a drink. If it a winner *must* be established, various solutions are employed. The simplest decider is that the two skips, or any member of their team delegated to do so, play a single stone each to draw the shot; aiming for the button. Lots are drawn or a coin tossed to decide who goes first, and any or all the members of a team may sweep up to the tee, but no-one may sweep behind it. Once the stone has come to rest it is measured by the umpire and removed from the house. The opposing team plays a stone and that too is measured, and the closer to the tee wins. A stone has to reach the house to count, and if neither reaches the process is repeated.

In finals or knockouts it is usual to play an extra end or ends until a winner is decided, but this is seldom done in club games because of the time factor. A quick solution where time is a factor is to count the number of ends each team has won, the higher being declared the winner. Sometimes, if the decision covers several games, the shots are counted, or shots up, or shots and ends. Whichever method is employed, it is wise to establish before the game what the rules are for every competition.

To establish an overall winner of a competition, whether over a weekend or an entire seaon, can be very complicated, especially if the organiser tries to be fair to everyone. The subject will be dealt with in more detail in the chapter on competitions.

Note: The use of the six-foot measure at the back line during play (i.e. before all sixteen stones have been played) is restricted to a measurement from the tee to the tangent between the back line and the centre line. This is only to see if a stone is actually biting the house, and therefore in play and not beyond the back line. All other cases of a stone being beyond the back line or still in play are resolved visually between the skips. As much of curling has its foundations built on mutual agreement, the business of measuring for the sake of it is unnecessary. It wastes time and is usually of no real consequence. When it is important and the rules allow it, measure, otherwise use common sense and keep the game flowing as smoothly as possible.

The Rink

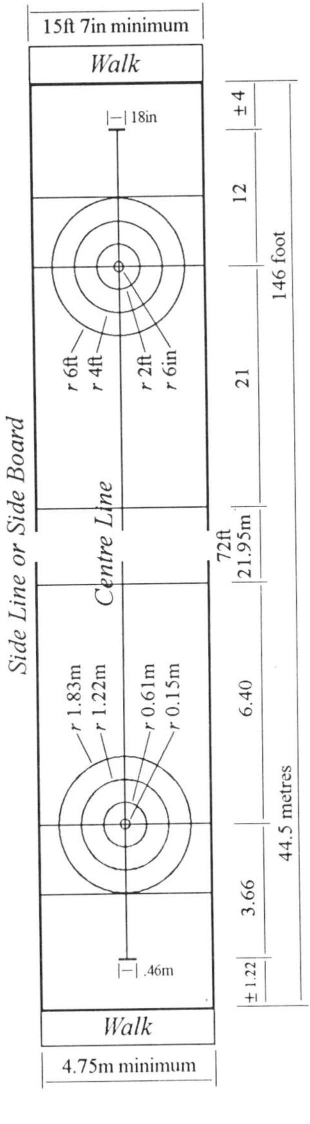
Foot Line & Hack
Back Line
Tee Line
Hog Line
Hog Line
Tee Line
Back Line
Foot Line & Hack
15ft 7in minimum
Walk
18in
r 6ft
r 4ft
r 2ft
r 6in
Side Line or Side Board
Centre Line
r 1.83m
r 1.22m
r 0.61m
r 0.15m
.46m
Walk
4.75m minimum
±4
12
21
72ft
21.95m
6.40
3.66
± 1.22
146 foot
44.5 metres

Sweeping Areas

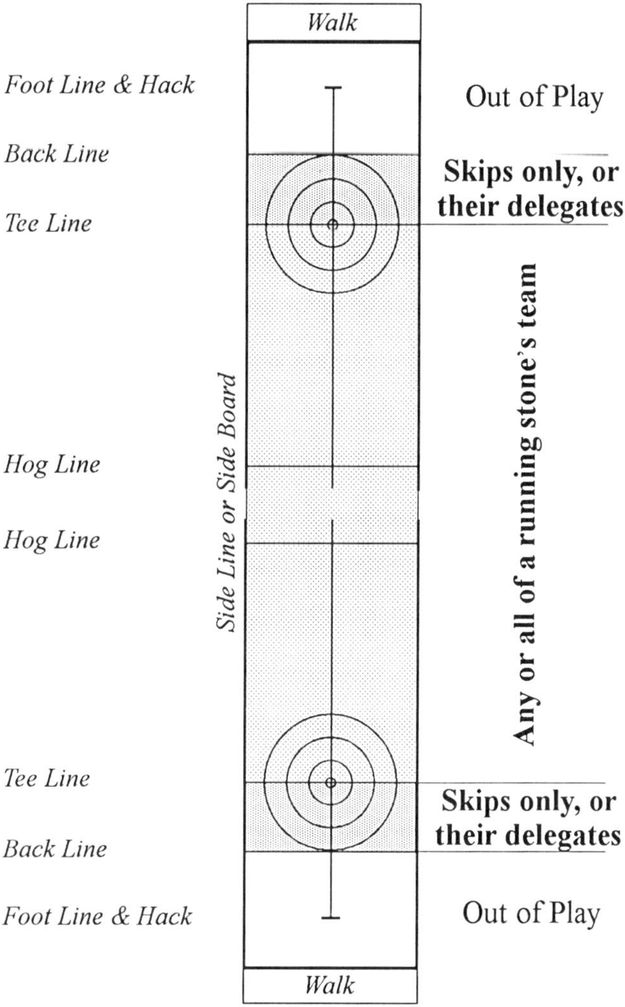

Equipment

The Ice

The most important piece of equipment in an ice rink is the floor. It would be easy to dismiss this statement as obvious, but the floor is so important that it must never be taken for granted. What the curler will see is a thin layer of ice with markings under it, but a great deal more goes into the preparation and maintenance of the ice and the base underneath than meets the eye.

The more modern ice rinks can have either a sand base or a concrete base, and these can have insulation beneath, rubble, gravel, or whatever was required to establish a firm foundation. Within the base will be a network of piping through which a coolant is pumped to freeze a layer of water. The skilled task of producing a good, smooth layer of ice is not simple and should not be underestimated.

There are few ice rinks in Scotland with sand bases, mainly due to its disadvantages. Older ice rinks still have sand bases which at the time of construction were considered adequate, but much has been learnt from the problems and better methods developed. The main disadvantage is that the rink is closed down for the summer, the ice melts to water and there remains only sand, which isn't firm enough for any alternative use without risking damage to the pipes within. The other disadvantage is permafrost, which is why the rink has to shut down for summer.

Permafrost is a serious problem, common in colder countries but not well understood here. When the coolant is pumped through the pipes it not only freezes the layer of sand and the water added on top, it also freezes the ground or layers below. Without insulation this freezing can be considerable, and because ice expands when it grows colder the foundation layers must try to absorb the changes, or the ice above will heave. Research has shown that the average depth of permafrost in a six-month season is seven feet, and in an eight-month season twelve feet. The depth of frost is very much influenced by the amount of moisture in the subsoil, but the problem cannot be ignored even in the best of circumstances.

Concrete floors were developed as a result, partly because they're more energy efficient and partly because they allow the rinks to be used for other purposes during summer. Also, with a good base that doesn't heave much the ice can be maintained during summer if desired, and with proper insulation the ice will not cause serious problems.

The typical construction of a concrete ice pad will have a heater pad on the subsoil to prevent permafrost. Six inches or more of insulation will separate the pad from the frozen area. The coolant pipes will lie on top of the insulation embedded in a layer of concrete, with the surface of the concrete levelled and smoothed. A well-run ice rink can have ice one week and a conference the next, melting and freezing almost at will, which helps tremendously towards the finances of the establishment.

The most cost-effective coolant which is pumped through the base is brine (because saltwater does not freeze as readily), which is cooled by varying methods through cooling plant nearby. The plant and its maintenance are expensive items which need replacement from time to time, and a leak anywhere in the system can be a costly business. To guarantee ice throughout the season – and ice fit enough to curl on – is a challenge to every iceman, and usually they get it right.

The making of good ice is essential both to the customer and to the survival of the rink as a successful business. It requires a sound program, a competent iceman and dedicated staff. The needs of every rink will vary, where some will provide facilities for skating or ice hockey as well as for curling, and these needs often conflict. But the basics don't vary much and every iceman aspires to perfection, and a sheet of ice which doesn't behave as expected will not have the iceman to blame.

The method of preparing and maintaining good curling ice works as follows. By cooling down the floor or sand for a period of forty-eight hours, or until the brine is at a temperature of at least -5°C, the temperature of the building is also cooled. Most of the moisture in the building will condense onto the floor and freeze, showing as a fine layer of ice. Water that is sprayed through a fine spray will freeze on contact with this layer, and water is sprayed on gradually until an even layer of ice is established across the entire pad. This method reduces excess load on the refrigeration plant, while also providing the ice pad with a good seal. Heavier floods of water can now be added until the ice is deemed suitable for painting.

The painting is very important, because it will be there until the ice is melted again. Because even clean water contains many impurities which rise to the surface during freezing, often leaving the ice surface greasy and discoloured, only careful preparation will produce a good result. To remove the impurities and help the paint to bond properly the surface is scraped with a mechanical ice cutter, such as most rinks now use for daily maintenance.

Ice is not naturally white, it is either the ice pad or the concrete which is painted white beneath. This is done either by spraying or flooding the pad with special water-based ice paint, or by using lime, or even by laying down a layer of white paper. The white can then be sealed in with fine sprays of water in preparation for the lines and circles.

Before laying down the markings the rink is measured out carefully according to the specified regulations in the rules (see pages 39,112). Measurements are checked as meticulously as possible, and as a tape measure can have some stretch in it over long lengths every care must be taken. The circles can be drawn and painted, or pre-made plastic circles can be used. All the other lines are now usually laid down with cotton tapes of varying widths, which are pulled to a straight line and laid in place before being sealed in again with fine spray.

Once all the markings are in place, floods of water are added to build up the depth of ice required. The finished level is scraped clean, brushed and mopped, after which the final finishing layer of fine pebble is applied. The hacks, normally made of rubber, are added – if they're loose blocks the holes are drilled which hold them in place. The centre holes are drilled, and curling can begin.

This process can take as long as two weeks to complete, depending on the machinery available and the facility's requirements. Regular scraping, sweeping, mopping and pebbling take place to maintain the surface at its best, and at periodic intervals the ice can be partially melted if required to overcome problems that occur. Should a hole be created (by banging a stone into the ice) it has to be carefully filled and scraped level, and heaving can cause much extra work for an already busy schedule. Considering that many ice rinks provide facilities from morning till late at night, the best ice is found in rinks where everyone respects the altogether precious surface.

Curling Stones

Curling stones are produced from very hard granite, which can withstand the great force endured when they strike together. Many of the curling stones around the world are produced from the granite of Ailsa Craig, a small rocky island at the mouth of the Firth of Clyde near Glasgow. Although the island is now a bird sanctuary and has a special scientific interest of breeding sea birds, quarrying still takes place at certain times of the year with minimal disturbance to wildlife. There are also stones produced from the granite Trevor, from Wales.

The lumps of rock are transported to a factory in Mauchline, Ayrshire. The pieces are then machined by professional tradesmen to the shape and weight that is standard throughout the world today. Although the stone can be heavy, weighing in at around 40lbs, it doesn't take a great deal of effort to deliver up the ice to the other end of the rink, due to the shape of the cup on each level surface and its running band.

Only this narrow rim of the cup actually touches the ice surface, which reduces the amount of friction between the stone and the ice. But it is the friction between the running band and the ice that causes the stone to curl, and if the running band were to wear smooth or become damaged there would not be predictable and reliable curl. In this case the stone would have to return and be redone with a new running band, along with the others in the set. Stones are now also made with an inset sole, which can be removed and replaced when necessary.

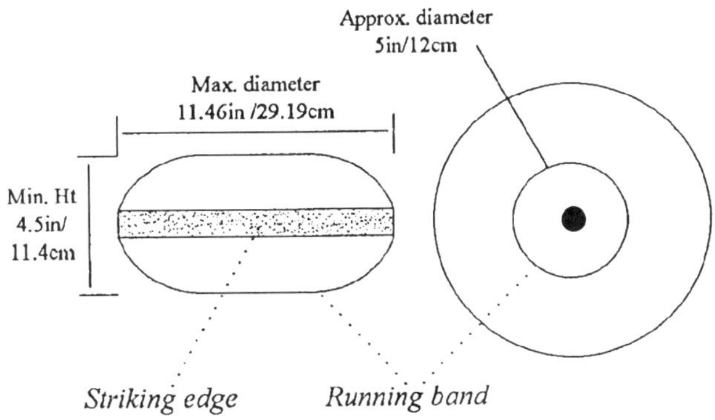

It can be clearly seen from the diagram, which has no handle included, that the stone is fully reversible – the handles are bolted on through the hole in the middle. The running band, only about an eighth of an inch (3mm) wide, is a most valuable part of the stone and could easily become damaged or worn, and by reversing the stone a new running band will be in use. Rinks regularly reverse the stones so that the running bands wear evenly, or a sudden change would prove too dramatic in its effect. Stones should also be stored on carpeting when not required, to protect the running band from damage.

Although the curling stones are very strong and heavy great care must be taken in the cleanliness of the ice surface. Should the stone collect a piece of dirt its rotation can easily be reversed and so its curl. Even a small hair from a broom or a piece of fluff from a jumper can affect the stone's progress, so delicate is its contact with the ice. Grit and dirt from outdoor shoes can also cause damage to the running band of the stone and it costs a great deal to repair.

The actual sizes of stones vary and even with every effort no two stones will be truly alike. If the granite used is of a higher density the stone could be heavier and should therefore be smaller to compensate; conversely if it is a lighter granite the stone will have to be thicker. So only the limits are specified: no heavier than 44lbs (19.96kg), no greater in circumference than 36in (91.44cm), or no wider in diameter than 11.46in (91.44cm), and a height of at least 4.5in (11.43cm). This leaves the stonemaker the problem of making a matching set as near as possible to each other in every respect, and if one of these should be broken in the rink it could prove difficult to replace.

Mini-stones are now available for use by youngsters at virtually all ice rinks. These stones are about half the weight of full-sized stones yet perform much the same, and they are a very good way for youngsters to develop their new skills. The stones are also made of granite, though plastic ones are made which are usually a little lighter still. Nothing teaches youngsters the fun of curling better than mini-stones.

Other equipment

For the beginner taking up curling most ice rinks will provide all the equipment needed. You need to bring your own *clean* pair of training shoes and wear warm, loose-fitting clothing. Only when you decide to curl on a regular basis will you consider buying your own shoes and brushes.

Curling shoes have one sliding sole and one grippy sole – if you are right handed the sliding sole is on your left foot and vice versa if you are left handed. There are many different types of shoes on the market, the more expensive ones usually of better quality and tending to last longer. Curling shoes are classed by the speed of the sliding sole, slow, medium or fast, and this is determined by the material and construction of the sole.

It is not always a good idea for a beginner to buy a fast curling shoe to start with. If you do not want to go to the expense of buying a pair of shoes you can get oversliders which simply slide over your trainers, but it would be advisable to contact your local ice rink coach or iceman for advice. Many beginners use ducting tape to carefully envelop the sole and edges of their sliding foot – it works exceptionally well and costs very little.

There are also slip-on kippers (anti-sliders) available, which many curlers use while sweeping to provide better stability on the ice when they prefer not to use a sliding foot. These kippers are also extremely useful to wear when you leave the ice, as they help to protect the sliding surface of your slippy sole and keep it clean.

Curling brushes come in all shapes, sizes and designs. The oldest is certainly the original straw broom, like a witch's broom, used by curlers throughout North America and Europe. To use them to good effect is a specialised skill and they need replacing at regular intervals, and have become almost obsolete. Nowadays curling brushes are produced with horse or hog hair bristles, but these do tend to drop hairs which then cause the problem of pick-ups on the ice. There are now new synthetic brushes with pads instead of bristles, or even pads over the bristles, which are light and easy to use and also resolve the problem of shedding hairs.

Whichever brush you buy will be a matter of personal preference. Cheaper brushes will have stiffer bristles, requiring more effort on the ice, while the more expensive ones with softer bristles will be a joy to use. The length of the handle is important (but can be changed quickly with a sharp saw!), as is the width of brushing surface. Ladies should try to find a narrow, soft brush with a shorter handle to aid them in the strenuous business of effective sweeping. Beyond these very few guidelines only experienced coaches and curlers will be able to advise individuals on their particular requirements.

Brushes should be kept clean. To maintain the quality of the bristles – and to remove loose hairs – it pays to wash them occasionally and, when they're not in use, to keep them wrapped in a plastic bag. When the bristles age they disintegrate, shedding tiny pieces of bristle all over the ice, and this must be kept a careful eye on. Shoes too need looking after, the leather will soon crack if it dries out and repairs can be a problem. Most regular curlers have a kitbag for their equipment and clothing, which goes a long way towards protecting their investment.

Curling clothing is becoming increasingly available, ranging from gloves, trousers, sweatshirts and jackets. It is helpful to everyone, as well as the quality of the ice, to choose clothing which doesn't shed fluff and to keep your clothing clean. What you wear will depend on your budget and preferences, but thin layers are better than thick and loose clothing better than tight.

Technique

When you know how something should be done it is possible to aspire to it. With proper tuition, application and practice you will soon be able to do it. To refine the action will simply take a little longer.

Technique in curling, as in any other activity, is designed to improve your ability, your consistency and your rate of success at playing your shots or sweeping those of others. This chapter is included here not only to help a total novice to get started in the game, but also to enable established curlers to improve on their abilities.

For reasons of safety, as well as health, it is a very important chapter and curlers will benefit from careful study. Not only does curling rely on fitness and physical effort towards the sweeping, it also requires suppleness and relaxation for the artistry of a gentle delivery. Looking after your body is as important as your technique.

Warming Up

Before going on the ice all curlers should get into the habit of warming up, so that the body is prepared for the action ahead.

- Always start with some aerobic exercise – jog, march, walk briskly, and this will get the blood pumping round the body and warm the muscles in anticipation of action.
- Do gentle mobilising exercises, putting the joints through their normal ranges.
- Stretch specific muscle groups to be exercised. Stretch and hold for fifteen seconds, and don't bounce.
- Always finish with a curling delivery stretch, and change legs so both sides are similarly stretched.
- Don't forget to do some similar exercises at the end of your game to cool down.

Specific Exercises

Heart:

Jog, jump or hop on the spot for about thirty seconds while swinging both arms freely.

Neck:

Move your head to each of the four quarters, holding the stretch. Do it a few times. *Do not circle.*

Shoulders and Back:

Do a few rope-pulls by stretching each hand in turn to the ceiling, as if being pulled up by a rope.

Sides:

Slide each hand in turn down your thigh, stretching your body sideways. Do it a few times.

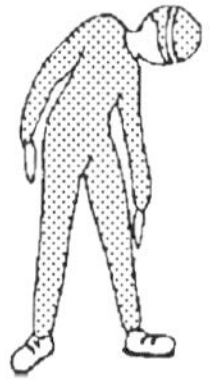

Front Thighs:

Pull each foot up in turn, pushing your pelvis forward and keeping your knees together. Do it a few times.

Calves:

Stand near a wall with front leg bent and rear leg straight, its heel on the ground, and press the hips forward. Change legs and do it a few times.

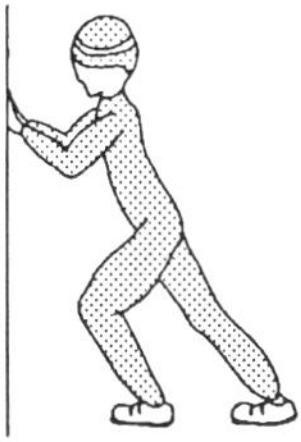

Back Thighs:

Sit on the floor with one leg straight and your hands clasping the other foot. Push to straighten the bent leg. Change legs and do it a few times.

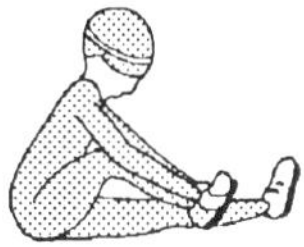

Slide:

Kneel on the floor, raise one knee with its foot flat on the floor. Ease bodyweight forward with both arms outstretched towards the floor, and stretch out the rear leg. Change legs and do it a few times.

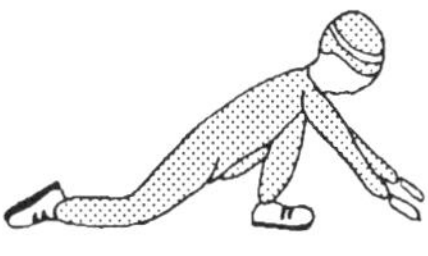

Delivery

The art of delivering a stone from the hack at one end of the rink to the target area at the other is all about balance and technique. Most new curlers can manage to send a stone somewhere up the ice – the skill is to develop a consistent delivery technique that will give direction and weight control to every shot played, with the desired result.

The stone must be delivered in an intended straight line from hack to target (the skip's brush), with the correct turn of the handle (in or out). Add to that the correct speed of sliding delivery up the ice so that, at release, the stone is travelling at the correct speed for the shot, and not being propelled at the last moment by an extra shove. However, a well-played stone is not totally dependent on your efforts alone, but is a combination of the skip's skill at giving the correct ice (direction) for the shot asked and the sweepers' efforts in guiding your stone to the exact destination.

Curling is a lot more fun when you understand the basic delivery. Throwing a curling stone is like swinging a golf club – line up to the target, press forward, smooth rhythmic backswing and forward swing, all with good balance and posture. It is graceful, relaxed, controlled and – when well executed – beautiful both to see and to do.

As a beginner it will be helpful to practise the delivery movements on dry land, which will help your confidence when you do take to the ice. It is a good idea to work up from a woolly sock over your shoe as a makeshift slider, to a plastic-bag slider, to a full-sole slider. Youngsters seem to have no bother at all, but beginners who are a little more advanced in years may be a little more conservative in their approach. It is amazing how quickly new curlers develop a balanced delivery with proper tuition and a little serious application.

There are two basic kinds of delivery, one with a pendulum backswing of the stone, where the stone leaves the ice, and one without, where it doesn't. To be as helpful as possible both will be dealt with here, one after the other.

Before you can do anything, be sure that you know in your mind exactly what the skip has asked you to do, and how you intend doing it. Clean your stone, set your mind and prepare for the line-up.

The Line-up

A correct line-up will go a long way towards eliminating problems in the delivery.

Approach the hack from behind and put the ball of your driving (gripper) foot securely on the hack, toe pointing to the brush, sliding foot forward and parallel and your body square towards the target. Your throwing arm will be straight and relaxed, while your other arm will be holding the brush.

Lower yourself into a comfortable sitting position, the brush woodside down on the ice with its handle under your arm, your hand about eighteen inches from the head. Sit up, keep your head up and your eyes focused on the skip's brush.

The skip doesn't always stand at the centre where it is easy to line up to the brush, but the same line-up drill must be used even if the target line is out in the wings and you must adjust your foot position in the hack to face the skip's brush square on. *Face his brush, not the centre line.*

Grip

The stone must be beside your driving foot, next to the hack on the centre line. Grip the handle with the middle of your fingers, resting it between the first and second joints. With your wrist high and palm off the handle, position your thumb on the inside of the handle. Keep this hand position throughout the whole movement.

For the clockwise turn point the handle to the ten-o'clock position – the stone will curl from left to right. Keep the handle pointing in this direction until the stone is released at the end of the slide. For the anti-clockwise turn point the handle to the two-o'clock position – the stone will curl from right to left.

Forward Press

Press your upper body, stone and brush forward in one smooth movement. Keep the stone and all motion on line to the skips brush, your throwing arm straight and relaxed. Now transfer your bodyweight onto both feet for the next step.

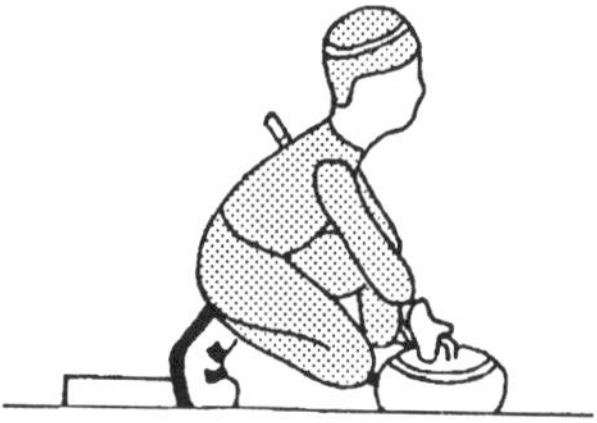

BACKSWING DELIVERY

Hip Lift

Lift your hips without straightening your legs completely. Do not lift your upper body, keep your head and shoulders above the stone and your throwing arm straight. Keep your head up with your eyes still on the skip's brush.

Backswing

The movement backwards starts with your hips, then stone and brush are pulled back. Put most of your weight onto the hackfoot as your sliding foot moves back, until the toe is level with the hackfoot.

Now swing the stone backwards with a pendulum motion; keep your upper body in position, head up and hack leg bent at the knee. Your throwing arm is still straight and relaxed, and your shoulders square to the target.

Forward Swing

Swing the stone forward to meet smoothly with the ice. The brush movement forwards should mirror the stone movement. Bring your sliding foot through under your chest, the toe turned slightly outwards, the foot directly behind the stone. Delay the leg drive until the stone is out in front of your body and on the line of delivery.

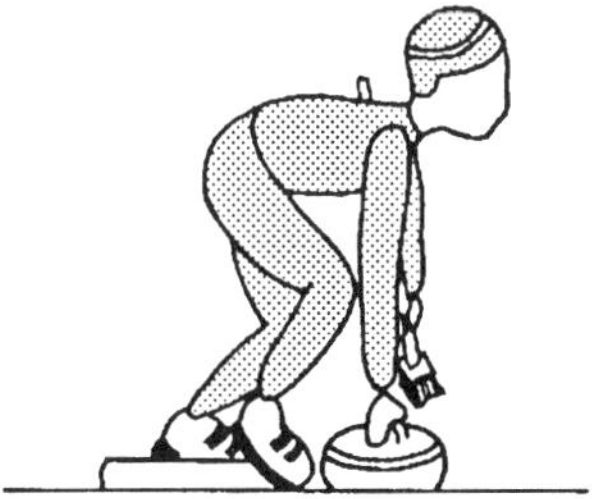

Transfer all your body weight slowly over the sliding foot and try not to lean on the stone. Lower your body during the slide with the trailing leg directly behind the sliding foot to act as a natural rudder. The throwing arm remains straight and relaxed throughout. It will be helpful to visualise the forward movement of stone and brush as pushing a wheelbarrow (or carrying a tray of drinks at arms length!).

The leg drive, as required, combined with the momentum of the stone will generate sufficient forward movement for you to leave the hack and slide smoothly down the ice towards your target.

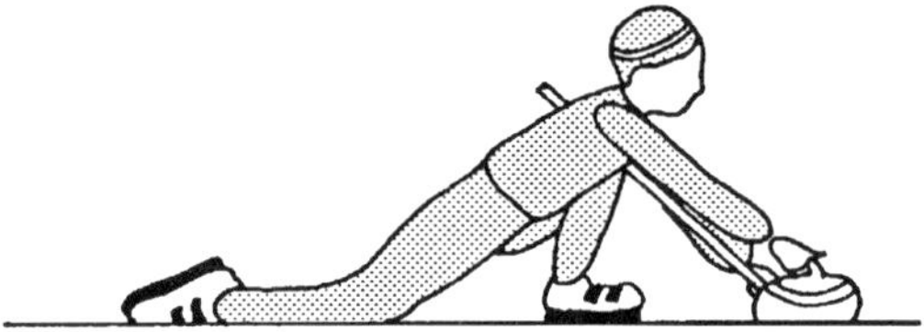

Handle and Release

The release is gentle and soft, and happens at the end of the slide. Your hand turns from the two-o'clock or ten-o'clock position to the twelve-o'clock position as it leaves the stone and moves to a handshake position above the stone on the target line. Your wrist is held high throughout the delivery and the turn is made above the centre of the stone, not at the end of the handle. The release should be smooth, clear and decisive.

Wait until your slide has come to its natural finish before you attempt to stand up. Remember to put your weight on your gripper foot first to raise your body to an upright position.

It is important that the entire sole of your sliding foot remains in contact with the ice during delivery, which improves balance and reduces stress on the knee, especially in the longer term when ligaments can be damaged.

NO–BACKSWING DELIVERY

With this delivery the stone remains on the ice at all times. The momentum gained by the stone in the backswing delivery is replaced by momentum from forward body movement and leg drive. The elimination of the back swing results in fewer balance problems. This delivery is ideal for young curlers who lack the strength to swing the stone, for beginners to the sport and for people with shoulder or back problems.

Line-up, Grip and Forward Press

These are the same as those described for the backswing delivery, except that the stone is placed directly in front of the hackfoot rather than beside it.

Hip Lift

Your legs lift your hips with upper body remaining parallel to the ice and the weight equally divided between your feet. Your hips stay low with legs bent to give more thrust out of the hack.

Back Movement

Pull the stone backwards towards the hackfoot. Move your hips back over the hack and shift your weight to the hackfoot. Move the sliding foot straight back to stop about a foot behind the hackfoot. Transfer your weight onto the sliding foot, sufficiently to re-establish your balance.

Forward Movement

As the stone is moved forward your body rocks forward. The sliding foot begins to move forward and your body weight is transferred back to the hackfoot, while the sliding foot moves in directly behind the stone. The hackfoot begins its forward push and your body lowers its weight onto the sliding foot.

Turn and Release

These are the same as for the backswing delivery.

In summary, for both deliveries, the stone and brush should be pulled back first, on line, followed by the sliding foot, to give a controlled backward movement. In the forward movement, the stone and brush should come first, then the foot, with hips dropping down into the sliding position. To emphasise this, think of *STONE–FOOT, STONE–FOOT.*

These two basic deliveries should get you started without many problems. Should you feel uncomfortable don't hesitate to get in touch with a qualified coach or attend a few coaching sessions, it helps very much.

It is important to remain confident and comfortable throughout, if you believe in your shot you'll play it well. Remember also that it is a swing of the stone, not a lift – strength is not what is required, but timing and finesse.

Sweeping

You will probably learn to sweep with a slippy sole on, and will naturally find it easier to sweep on the side that makes your leading foot the one with the slippy sole. Remember that it is not essential to stay on a slippy sole throughout the duration of a game, if you feel more comfortable with your kipper on (i.e. with two gripper feet), then do so. You may also find it preferable to sweep on the other side, and this is a definite bonus to your team. It is in fact a good thing to be a competent sweeper on both sides – it makes the sweeping much more effective as the brushes are closer together, it gives both sweepers room to move and both will have a clearer view of stationary play near the head.

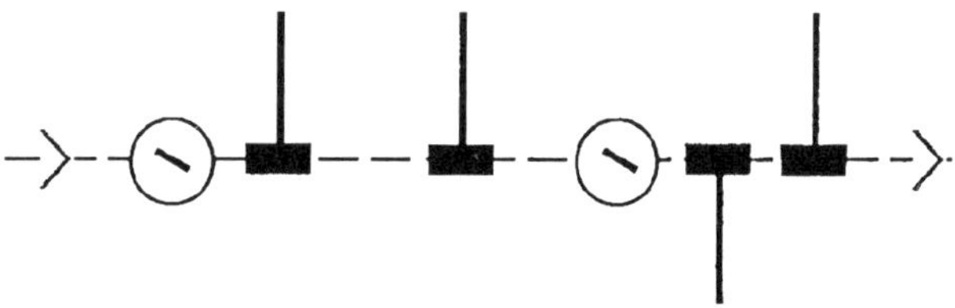

Why We Sweep

- To remove any dirt or debris which would affect the path of the stone.
- To allow the stone to travel farther by momentarily warming the ice. Hard sweeping creates a thin film of water under the stone that acts as a lubricant. Some even say that fast sweeping close to a stone creates a differential in air pressure which aids the stones momentum. It is certainly true that good sweeping can make a stone travel six to ten feet farther, especially on keen ice.
- To allow a running stone to travel straighter for longer.

The Brush

There are many styles of brush and choosing one is a matter of personal preference (see page 47). Most ice rinks supply brushes which will be perfectly adequate for beginners, but try out as many different ones as you can before buying.

The most important part is the head, the bit that touches the ice. The different types of brush have different levels of friction with the ice, and so has the width of the brush. It is no use to try and sweep a length of ice with a brush that is too heavy to handle, and only the very strong and fit can sweep properly with a twelve-inch brush. It is also essential that the entire sweeping surface of the brush is in contact with the ice, even for light sweeping. Remember that all brushes should be kept clean.

Sweeping rules

Refer to the diagram on page 40 for the areas where sweepers can sweep. The general dos and don'ts are only to sweep your own running stone, never to touch a stone, never to dump rubbish in front of it and not to sweep beyond the tee line unless you're a skip or his delegate. The full rules are dealt with in the chapter starting on page 111.

How to Sweep

Sweep with great care and with all your heart, it is a skill as difficult to master as drawing the button. Only practice can make perfect, but sweeping a stone to perfection is most satisfying and essential for a winning game.

Grip

Place one hand palm up about one third way down the handle. Place the brush handle under your arm, held in against the body; place the other hand palm down about two thirds down the handle. Lean forward and press down with both hands to apply pressure on the brush head as required. The more pressure, the more friction, the more effect – the more tiring it is.

Stance

Keep your body at 45° so that you can easily watch where you are going, and face down the ice towards your skip in the house. Your feet should be slightly more than shoulder width apart with your knees bent. Lean forward at the waist so that most of your weight is over the leading foot and use your gripper foot to generate the paddling movement. Always keep an eye open for stationary stones, your feet will have to negotiate a way past when you reach them.

Footwork

WITHOUT SLIDER

Using the stance described, jog or sidestep down the ice while sweeping ahead of the stone. With this method you can position yourself on either side of the stone, but it does use more energy and can become tiring during a hard game. Apply pressure on the brush head while sweeping across the path of the stone.

WITH SLIDER

This is referred to as the push-slide method, and allows the curler to keep up with the stones while sweeping in a controlled manner. It requires a slider on the sweeper's forward (sliding) foot and a gripper on the rear (pushing) foot. Using the stance as described put most of your weight on your sliding foot and push with your gripper foot while allowing the sliding foot to glide. To increase the speed of your slide lengthen the stroke of your pushing foot. Try to develop a rhythm that suits you, so that you're able to sweep with fast strokes at any speed. Do your best not to have your legs on the line between the player and his stone, so that he can clearly see its progress.

Sweeping

An effective sweeping stroke requires a combination of speed and pressure. Move the brush head quickly across the stone's path (speed) while applying weight (pressure) on the head of the brush. The arms should be bent and the brush gripped firmly, but not too tightly. The sweeping stroke must finish to either side of the stone and cover the full width of the stone's path (see Rules, page 120).

Partner sweeping

Usually there are two sweepers working together. The sweeper closest to the stone is responsible for judging the speed of the stone, he is also usually the more experienced and/or the better sweeper. The speed (weight) is judged by constantly monitoring the distance between the stone and the target.

Always be ready at the hack when your team is preparing to deliver a stone. As a sweeper always watch to see what shot is indicated by the skip, so that you know exactly what is required. Move forward in combination with his delivery but out of his way, and try to have equal speed to that of his stone. Respond quickly when asked to sweep – if you are not ready to sweep there will be piercing looks all round. You can sweep from tee line to tee line so don't give up as you approach the house. Always travel up the ice with the stone in case you are needed – the stone might be deflected and the skip will have to adjust his plan. When sweeping close to the stone be careful not to touch it – if you do so own up immediately to your skip.

Watch all the draw-weight stones carefully, and with experience you will learn to judge the weight (speed) required for a stone to reach the intended distance. You will learn to note when a stone is light (short) or heavy (long). Communicate with your partner and keep the skip informed of your judgements – it will help the skip with his decisions on sweeping. Use your judgement when you can, but always be alert to counter instructions. The skip's calls are on/off, sweep/up, yes/no, hurry/whoa, or any mixture of these and many others. Learn to recognise your skip's voice and favourite calls so that you hear correctly and save yourself those piercing looks.

When you've done your sweeping, the job is not yet done. Make your way back to the delivery end, catch your breath, forget the previous stone and concentrate on the next – it will need sweeping too. Good sweeping is an essential ingredient in making accurate and precise shots. Sweepers perfect the shots, and sweeping is what makes curling a team effort.

The Team

A curling game of high standard depends above all on the team. No individual can win a good game on his own and no single player can claim the credit.

How difficult it is for the beginner who steps onto the ice for the first game he has ever played, to have to play twenty stones and only get one or two near to where the skip wanted, to sweep badly and get it all wrong, and then to step off the ice a winner yet knowing he's not contributed at all. Worse still if the game has been lost, for surely he is entirely to blame – not so, for it is a team effort. The team shares the credit *and* the blame, and the beginner is not there to play a perfect game, but to do his best. Get this right, and remember it for ever.

The team is like the eight spokes of a wagon wheel, each member responsible for two; the sweeping is the rim and the skill of the skip is at the hub. This single unit is strong and can well cope with a missing spoke or two if the others can take the strain and the hub doesn't fail. The single most important task every spoke must perform is its best, in its turn, at the moment when it is called into action. More simply, play the stone in your hand. Forget the glory, the brilliant shot on television, the opposing player's perfect stone, your own previous not-so-perfect stone – play only the stone in your hand. Understand what is needed, visualise the shot, decide your line and weight, relax, concentrate and play it to perfection. It works.

It is unfortunate, but inevitable, that beginners are given the position of lead as their baptism. It is a very important position that can easily make or break a game, and the shots required are difficult to play with any degree of consistency. But where else does a player learn more than at lead? Every single player starts at lead and works his way up from there to second and third and perhaps skip. Be patient, it takes time, but if you practise a little and learn well it comes, and there are still many skips who enjoy playing lead occasionally for the valuable practice they gain.

As a direct, and intended, consequence of the Free Guard Zone rule, skips will now virtually always ask the lead to put a stone in that zone, a few feet short of the house. Whether he asks for one on the centre line or to either side will depend on his tactics. At the start of a game the ice will often be dour and frosty, with the stones needing a few pounds extra weight to reach the hog line, and part of the skip's thinking will be to test the weight and line. Play the weight and line he asks and he will learn something, even if you fail, and he will be very happy if you succeed. A guard anywhere in that zone is worth something, because the opposition cannot simply knock it out.

The opposing lead will try to put a stone in there too, and your skip now asks you to draw around it into the house. When the opposing lead plays, keep your mind on *his* weight and line, because more often than not you will be asked to follow the shot with a better one. You play your draw shot with a little more line and a little more weight, but not too much, and the sweepers will do their best to work the stone into place. If you're too heavy it will be out the back and that is plain useless; if you're tight on the brush and knock the free guard out it is equally useless; if you're light and don't reach it is a little better and even if you tap the guard up it is better – the best is to visualise what he wants and play the shot as well as you can. You will feel extremely good when you shave the guard and sit protected behind it, and your team will raise their brushes in praise. Even the opposition will raise their brushes, because you have done well – but so have the sweepers and the skip.

The opposing lead has played too heavy and sits in the house, and your skip wants you to knock it out. *Nae bother*, you think, but you feel terrified because you've never played a takeout before. Don't worry, because a takeout is easier than a dead-weight draw. The skip will give less ice and want more weight, probably no more than hack weight, and as long as you're on the brush something will work. If you're off the brush nothing is likely to come of it and the next stone will guard the target, with your team struggling for the rest of the end. Visualise weight and line, relax, and be on the brush. Do your very best not to be light, because the skip has not asked you to guard the opposition's stone – all he wants is a heavy draw.

After two or three ends you find your length. Everyone calls it beginner's luck but the stones are appreciated all the same, and your wily skip recognises your strength and asks you time after time for exactly the same boring shot. You play as he asks, but the stones suddenly keep going out the back. You don't know why, you're still playing the same weight and no matter how hard you try the stones simply will not stop. Welcome to curling.

Ice changes. What was frosty has been swept to a high polish, and with only the polished pebbles to slide on stones travel very much farther down the ice – and out the back. Humidity and temperature play a part too, as do constant sliding down the same track and stones played along the same line. One half of the rink can be keen and the other slow; the centre can be slippy and the sides dour; a single missing light bulb overhead can make a difference, as can the number of curlers on the ice. Players learn to compensate and do so very quickly, but it can be frustrating at first and beginners have to learn to be patient. Develop a good, constant slide with excellent balance and, with practice, the rest will fall into place.

Playing second can seem like a waste of time, compared to lead, but the second has to compensate for or consolidate on what the lead has played. If there's nothing in or near the house he now has to play the perfect guard, only more perfect than the lead because it can be knocked out. Or he has to knock out opposing stones before they can consolidate with guards, or draw around a guard, or guard a stone in the house. The variety of shots required from a second is higher than from a lead and he has to be able to play them at any given time – no chance here to practise until he finds his length, he has to know from experience and get it right first time. His takeout stones will often need to be at strike weight, so his line needs to be very accurate. He will definitely need to be experienced at lead and therefore one step up, but the lead will still have the upper hand on exact draw weight.

Both lead and second are vital as sweepers. Not only must they learn to sweep every stone effectively at any weight, but they need to tell when a stone needs sweeping for weight or not. As they do most of the sweeping and do so side by side they soon mould into one half of the team, each feeding off the other for energy and motivation when the muscles start burning, constantly communicating whilst sliding beside a stone to evaluate its progress. Good sweeping is as valuable as any good stone, but good judgement of its progress is more valuable – without good judgement sweeping is often a waste of time. There is no law that says they must be young and fit either, because it is judgement and effective sweeping that count more than fitness, but fitness certainly helps when it is a tight game on dour ice.

A problem often encountered in curling at club level is the progress, or lack of progress, of sweepers returning down the ice to be ready for the next stone. The accepted area where they should be is between the hog lines and along the side lines, and definitely not in the house or the guard zone. Nor should they be behind the house in the line of play, or trying to have a conversation with the skip who wants to concentrate on the next stone, or have a banter with each other across the rink and step ever closer to be able to hear. Standing around the opposition at the delivery end is allowed, but only if their play is not affected – having a few words across the player's stone will soon cause tension and develop into a very poor game of curling.

It is very courteous, and good sense, to develop the habit of either standing still along the side lines between the hog lines while the opposition is playing, or making your way back along the side lines in such a way as to not interfere with the opposition's play. Most good sweepers will do their job, turn and slowly make their way back, relaxing as they do so, and be ready to sweep afresh as soon as their player addresses his next stone; they will say very little to interfere with his effort unless asked, and will do their very best to get that stone to where the skip wants it. That is what sweeping is about.

The third is the player who must keep the team out of trouble. More often than not he will play takeouts to clear opposing stones or guards and so give his skip a chance to win the end. Sometimes he will have to play very precise guards to close ports or protect a good position. On occasion he might even be in such deep trouble that a heavy strike is called for to totally rearrange the head, removing several stones in the one blow. A good third is accurate, calm and consistent, but above all he is accurate.

When the skip has to play his stones the third must take his place in the house, and for that period the third has control in the house and only he can sweep behind the tee. As the other half of the team the skip and third will have good communication between them and will both know the strategy being pursued at the time, and when they discuss the next shot they will want to do so in peace. Although lengthy discussions can wear the lead and second down they have to be endured, for there is no hurrying the skip or third. Problems like those are discussed afterwards, not on the ice.

And then there is the skip. He's the person you more than likely will forget about, because he's at the other end of the ice all the time and you'll hardly exchange more than a very few words with him. *Who* needs *him*! You know the shots you want to play and they're not what *he* is asking for, and he never gives you enough ice anyway! And why does he shout sweep all the time when you *are* sweeping as hard as you can already, why doesn't he come and help!

All true, but only from your own point of view. The skip is the hub of the wheel, the person with the job of holding the unit together and on course for a good performance. He is more abstracted from the shots, has a different perspective and can evaluate their progress better, both for line and weight, and he can be good at it. Because he isn't being pumped full of adrenaline by the sweeping he has time to study the ice, where the trouble spots are and where a helpful run develops. He soon reads the ice and knows how much draw there is, and consequently how much ice to give at all the different weights.

He also has a plan in his head. He is going to try this and that, and if they don't work he'll have another plan. As the stone comes towards him he'll see what the result is likely to be and, if it's not what he asked for, he'll adapt his plan and make the best of a poor stone. He'll shout sweep and you'll sweep, and he'll keep shouting because he's trying to help you by blasting you with extra energy, but if he's wise he'll be sure not to have you sweep when it won't do any good. When he has to and can safely leave the house he'll come and help you sweep, particularly if a stone *has* to reach the house, and he'll be very good at it.

Support your skip to the full, and you'll have a good team. His is the responsibility for every stone his team plays, as well as the opposing stones once they reach the tee line. He has to know the rules and interpret them wisely, and not always literally. He has to ensure that the game flows smoothly and must bring the best out of his team, without hindering the opposition in their play. Above all he has to ensure that his team wins, even when they're hopelessly behind, and with full support from his team he can often perform miracles.

A good skip is calm and confident. He understands the game and its objectives, and he has progressed to the position of skip over several years because he loves the game. He can play any shot well and draw to the button with deceptive ease. He is usually a natural leader who believes in teamwork – he should never be an egotist playing only for a win to boost his own self. In all curling circles there are many legendary skips whom anyone would like to curl with for the honour; there are also a few successful skips who struggle to put a team together, because they really don't want a team.

When the lead plays rather poorly the second can still compensate, and the third can rescue a desperate situation with one good shot. The skip, given the slightest chance, can secure the end with skill, daring and finesse. He has nerve, confidence, concentration, finely honed ability. But the skip is human and will make mistakes, the end will be lost and the struggle a little harder. The best way to compensate for a poor skip stone is to play the perfect lead stone in the next end and build on it – before long the skip will take a big end of three or four and his poor shot will be forgotten, as will yours. Keep the wheel turning smoothly with each helping the other, and the team will play well; criticise each other throughout the game and the spokes will break, one by one.

When clubs decide their teams for the coming season they use a tried and tested method which had served them well in the previous years. A few knowledgeable folk will sit down and make the decisions, but you'll only see the results and will probably feel let down. Unfortunately a club has only so many members and they all have to be placed in teams, and the teams competing against each other have to be reasonably well balanced in ability to make the club's league a successful one. Whatever position you're placed in, remember that the skip has the right to change it before a game – if the club says you're lead but the skip says you're third, the skip wins. Don't despair, your abilities will be valued once you've developed them.

If you're unfortunate enough to find yourself in a club where a few members of long experience refuse to give you credit where it's due, you have a simple choice. You can learn to compromise and develop relationships upon which you can build, like the rest of the world tries to do, or you can change clubs. If you change clubs, remember that you will start as lead again, whether you're skip material or not, and you will have the same problems.

The same selection process usually happens in the other leagues, where the club often only appoints the skips who then have to find their own teams. These skips can even pass the game to another skip, should they have something better to do – more likely they will have another game on somewhere else and can't do both, as is often the case. This system is a natural progression of team selection where the skips now have the responsibility of choosing their own teams, and more often than not they'll stick to the same few players with whom they feel they do well. Keep improving with more practice and who knows, you might get asked next time.

When it comes to competitions the same applies, a skip puts a team together and enters to win – or at least have a few good games. The more serious the competition the more serious the selection, and soon the team will stick together for several years and acquire a few trophies along the way. For those who progress this far it is as well to remember that practice ice is expensive, as are competitions and travelling, but it is good practice to accept an opportunity if at all affordable. A bonspiel is what curling is all about and with a good team is tremendously enjoyable, and the experience will soon have you wanting more.

The majority of curlers – the backbone of curling – use the game for its original purpose of social relaxation during winter. They are quite happy to curl once a week or less and while some improve a little others don't seem to. When curling as a team becomes more important than curling as a club a dividing line appears; when competition becomes more important than playing the percentages in club games you are entering the domain of the sport. Should you do well they'll be pleased, for the club, and they'll always enjoy having you back for a game or two. But curling as a game is not curling as a sport, and a team in the game is a brotherhood of friends, not a fighting unit to win at any cost.

On the Ice

Curling is a game of sportsmanship, courtesy, politeness and good manners. Everyone who enjoys curling says so and there are two million of them.

Virtually every ice rink now provides coaching for beginners as well as more experienced curlers. They will be well qualified and any curler's game will benefit from their contribution. There are also vastly experienced curlers who teach the coaching staff, and the advice of these experts cannot be ignored. Here is what the experts say on etiquette:

Your behaviour on the ice is very important – poor behaviour and bad sportsmanship reduces everyone's enjoyment of the game, and is not likely to improve your own or your team's performance.

DON'T

- Don't lift your stone to clean it, just turn it over on the ice.
- Don't damage the ice by banging it with your brush or crashing your stone into it.
- Don't lie on, sit on or hold your hands on the ice for long.
- Don't move or talk when anyone is playing a shot.
- Don't talk to the player in the hack – it is distracting.
- Don't go into the circle unless you're sweeping up to the tee line, only the skips or their delegates are allowed.
- Don't stand behind the circle while play is in progress.
- Don't try to assist the skip in the house.
- Don't smoke or drink on the ice.
- Don't touch a running stone, if you do remove it from play.
- Don't touch a stationary stone, if you do tell the skip.
- Don't cross in front of a running stone or a player about to deliver a stone.
- Never criticise the skip or your team mates on the ice and especially not to the opposition.
- Leads and seconds only give opinions when asked by the skip.

DO

- Arrive in good time, change your shoes and be ready for your game.
- Introduce yourself to the opposition and shake hands.
- Stand still against the side lines when opponents are playing.
- Allow the opposition a clear view of their running stone.
- Be back at the hack ready to play when your turn comes.
- Always clean your stone before delivery.
- Always think on the hack before delivering a stone.
- Keep your eye steadily on the brush until your stone is under way – learn not to look at your stone.
- Follow through with your hand in the exact direction of the brush – teach your body to follow your eyes.
- Be ready beside your player when it is your turn to sweep.
- Sweep across the path of a stone and as close to it as you safely can.
- Sweep a stone if you think it's light, but communicate and listen for the skip's instructions.
- Follow the stone all the way to the house, you may be asked to sweep again.
- Watch every stone and learn what you can regardless of your position.
- Always sweep hard – tickling the ice is useless.
- Praise good shots and say nothing about "the others".
- Shake hands and socialise afterwards.
- Always remember the skip is in charge on the ice.

Arriving on time for your game, or ahead of time, is important. Most curlers lead busy lives yet they make the effort – obviously they think it's important too. A few have difficulty being on time for anything and for them there are penalties in the rules. But it is the whole team that is penalised, and that is clearly unfair to the other members of your team and very poor manners. If you are delayed please do phone the ice rink with a message, the staff will pass it on to your team and the game can go ahead without you.

Clothing needs careful consideration, and *you have to bring your own.* All regular curlers have their regular outfit based on what they've discovered suits them best. The experts say:

Footwear:

- Bring clean, flat-soled shoes (don't walk dirt onto the ice).
- Rubber or crepe soles are good – try tennis shoes or trainers.
- If in doubt, bring more than one pair to experiment.
- When you become experienced, invest in a slippy sole or proper curling footwear.

Trousers:

- Stretch, or loose-fitting trousers are essential.
- Tracksuit bottoms that don't shed fluff are good.
- Jeans are usually too tight for comfort.

Clothing:

- Several thin layers of close-knit fibric – you'll be working hard and will soon warm up.
- Heavy coats are not necessary and can be a nuisance.

Gloves:

- If your hands tend to get cold.
- They do help to keep your hands off the ice.

It is the best possible advice for players to do some aerobic and stretching exercises before playing a game, particularly if they are energetic players. Looking after your body is as important as looking after the ice and equipment, and if your muscles are not functioning properly good balance will be difficult to achieve, whether sweeping or delivering. Serious injury is a direct result of a careless approach to curling, ice is slippery and must be treated with respect.

For those who don't normally get much exercise, it is a very good idea to get just a little in the days before a game. Warm up with easy jogging on the spot for ten minutes, then gently stretch for about seven seconds per muscle group *without bouncing.* You'll be far less stiff afterwards if you invest a little time beforehand, and with a little preparation before the game you'll be well prepared to give your best.

Always step onto the ice with your grip foot, not your sliding foot, and avoid bumping into others. First learn to move about on the ice by a method of paddling, which means sliding on your slippy foot while paddling yourself forward on the grip foot and using your brush for balance. For a game players are allowed to have a practice slide from the hack without a stone in their hand, but it is proper courtesy to slide at a slight angle away from the centre line and not along it.

Before the teams step onto the ice the positions of play are decided. The two leads toss a coin and the winner asks his skip whether they go first or second. With very few exceptions the skip will choose to go second, in order to retain the last-stone advantage. Everyone shakes hands and wishes one another a good game, whether it is a bit of fun or the finals of a major championship. The skips move to the house, the playing skip takes up his position and indicates what he wants, while the other skip stands aside to await his turn. The team who plays first has the choice of which colour stones they will play with, the lead plays his first stone and the sweepers follow it down the ice, usually having to sweep.

At this early stage some useful pieces of information can be checked. The first and most obvious is whether the ice has been pebbled. There might be evidence of water droplets on the hack or the backboard, or the pebble will be clearly visible on the ice with a slightly brighter reflection. Make sure all the lights are on – managers and their hardworking staff are human and sometimes forget to switch on those for a particular sheet which had not been in use. Look for frost on the surface of the ice, a clear indication that the ice will be dour at the start. The start of the session is normally indicated by the ringing of the bell, and the bell will signal the end of the game. If the bell does not ring, the session will end on time as displayed by the rink clock. If any of these has not been done, let the skip deal with it before the game.

A very important point, especially at the start, is to clean the bottom of each stone before delivery. Often the parking area of the stones has collected loose dirt and/or frost and if the hack area isn't kept clean, this dirt will find its way onto the sheet of ice. A running stone will easily collect any debris under its running band and be deflected. Therefore, before addressing *each* delivery, turn the stone on its side and clean the bottom, sweep the dirt well aside and then prepare for the shot.

In the same vein is the care of your brush. After sweeping a stretch of frosty ice the bottom of your brush will be white with the stuff, and on dirty ice there will be several bits of dirt which you cannot see. Take the brush routinely to the side or preferably beyond the back boards and flick the frost and dirt off the hairs. It helps to keep the ice clean and will prevent many an unwanted pick-up. If you look at the surface of the brush against the white of the ice you'll also spot loose hairs before they actually fall off, and remove them before they ruin the skip's last stone. Remember that you are only allowed to take one brush into a game for sweeping – you can take another for delivering stones, but that usually only happens in serious competition.

At the completion of each end the stones in play have to be cleared to the back board and "parked". It is not a good idea to shove them at speed vaguely in the right direction, the stones are heavy and injuries can easily be the result. The norm is to take a stone or two and shepherd it with your brush, to keep it under control. It is a good habit to park the stones in numbered sequence, so that each player plays with the same two stones throughout – no two stones are truly alike. The lead must always be ready to play his first stone as soon as possible so as not to unduly delay the game, and he must not be expected to park and arrange stones as well as prepare for his delivery.

Skips have to signal the shot to be played, its intended line, its hand (turn) and its weight. Skips also call the sweeping both for line and weight, especially if a stone has not been delivered as expected, and sweepers must always be aware of changes in plan which only the skip can judge. Players soon grow accustomed to the signals individual skips might use, but there is a standard which should be followed. The general rule from the player's point of view is to ask the skip if you're not sure what he wants, or ask the sweepers if you've missed the instructions, but be sure you know what he wants and think carefully before you play. It is no use to argue afterwards because you missed the signals, or didn't understand them. Here are the signals a skip may give:

In-Turn Hand (clockwise)	Hold out the right hand (for right-handed players).
Out-Turn Hand (anti-clockwise)	Hold out the left hand (for right-handed players).
Draw Shot	Point with the brush to where the stone is to come to rest.
Guard	Hold the brush shoulder-high and parallel to the ice.
Freeze	Same as a draw, and tap the top of the brush with the free palm.
Raise	Point with the brush to the stone to be moved, then to where it must be moved.
Hit and Roll	Point with the brush to the stone to be removed, then to where the played stone is to roll.
Strike	Point with the brush to the stone to be removed, then indicate the weight to be played (see *Weight*).
Weight	Point to the back line if the shot is to be played at a weight to reach the back of the house, to the hack if it should be faster and to the barrier for faster still. Barrier weight shots may also be signaled by drawing the hand across the waist, and a strike by touching the shoulder.
Stones Lying	Point to opponent's stones with the handle and outwards with your free hand; for your own stones point with the brush, and your hand inwards towards your chest.
Sweeping	The Skip's call for sweeping is SWEEP or HURRY or YES or ON.

Not Sweeping — The Skip's call to stop sweeping is WHOA or UP or NO or OFF.

Tap Up — Hold your hand across the top of the brush – the distance of the hand from the top of the brush will show how much the target stone has to be moved.

As the game progresses, be alert and ready to play your stones when your turn comes. It will normally be the case that only two players are at the delivery end, the others are either sweeping or returning, and there should be no need for you not to be ready. It is helpful for the lead or second to have the skip's stone ready to play when he comes, it will save only a little time but will help his concentration a lot. It will also give him that unspoken token of support which will boost his confidence and make him feel good, and every skip deserves that at least.

The first ends can be unpredictable. The players are as yet unfamiliar with the ice, and it takes a little time to warm up and settle into the game. Always try to keep your weight up and give the stone a chance – if the rink is frosty the sweeping can be very hard work and stones frequently will be reluctant to reach the hog line. Watch also for changes in the ice. Whichever team settles first can easily take a few shots on the first end, and another three on the second end to rub it in, but if the struggling team can fight back this deficit can be clawed back. Never say die, not from the very first stone to the last. Here are some helpful hints from the experts:

- Curling is a team game – if a team member has an off day the other three should play just that little bit better to cover up.
- The art of good play – play the brush and the correct weight.
- An orthodox delivery makes "hitting the brush" easier and improves consistency.
- Know what weight is expected and play accordingly.
- Concentrate hard to find draw weight and then to keep it for ten ends.

- Remember that the first end or two will usually need more weight than normal.
- On keen ice good sweepers can take a stone 12 – 15ft farther.
- Good sweeping helps to keep a running stone straight.
- Concentrate hard when sweeping to be able to judge the weight of running stones.
- There are three variations to any shot – always try to play the best. For example:

  When asked to come to a stone in the house

  Best – freeze tight against it.
  Second best – tap it back a little.
  Worst – guard it and do the opposition a favour.

  When asked to play a strike on swingy ice

  Best – on the brush.
  Second best – wide, but it could draw enough.
  Worst – tight, because it will draw too much and miss.

  When asked to play a strike on straight ice

  Best – on the brush.
  Second best – tight, but it won't draw much.
  Worst – wide, because it won't draw much and miss.
- Tips for individual positions:

  For the front end (Lead and Second):

  - Never question the skip's ice.
  - Never question what the skip is about to play.
  - Return to the hog line after sweeping a stone.
  - Do not walk two abreast down the ice.
  - Concentrate on the game – always be ready, whether to sweep or to play.
  - Do not complain loudly about the opposition – send complaints via your third to the skip.

  For Thirds:

  - Be diplomatic as you must carry messages between the skip and front end.
  - Be able to assist the skip if asked – learn the ice at every opportunity as this will also help with your judgement of the skip's stones. Let him use you to bounce off his ideas and thinking, it helps you both.

- Take care when joining the skip behind the head, so as not to interfere with the opposition.
- Be competent with the various measures.

For Skips:

- Do not move when the opposition is about to play.
- Always be ready to sweep behind the tee.
- Never indicate that your player is off the brush, unless asked. Tell your third quietly in case the player asks, and so that the third learns the ice.
- Acknowledge shots played or attempted.
- Keep skipping and your own play apart if you are having a bad game.
- If the shot was well played but the ice wrong, let your player know.
- Settle the shot and the ice with your third before leaving the head.

Strategy in club curling varies from player to player, but there are a few obvious ways to start an end. A skip can try to guard either the middle of the house or the sides, and his choice will depend on a variety of considerations. It is wise to use the Free Guard Zone or have a stone just biting, but a stone past the tee line is seldom constructive. Stones in the wings have their uses, but stones in the middle have better potential. Ideally however they should lie in front of the tee line, or the opposition can draw up to them and lie quite safely holding shot. On the other hand if they're only just biting the outer circle the opposition could try to lie behind them, but these exacting draws are not easy and a stone on the edge can be very useful later in the end for a raised shot.

It is generally considered good strategy to leave the middle of the house open if you have last stone, but occupied if you don't have last stone – the latter giving you the best chance to steal the end by shutting your opponent out. Try to score *at least* one shot if you have last-stone advantage, and to limit the opposition to one shot only, *and no more,* when you don't have last stone. "Ones and twos and you'll never lose", but no-one will say no to a gift of more. It is certainly a case of being alert to the opportunities and always be ready to make the most of them.

The experts offer the following advice to skips on the subject of strategy:

- A skip should regularly consider the following when deciding upon strategy:
  - Who has last-stone advantage.
  - Which end it is and how many ends will be played.
  - What is the score.
  - How reliable or difficult are the ice conditions.
  - How well is his team playing.
  - What type of game does the opposition like to play (and how to avoid it).
- Play to the front of the house. A light stone ending as a guard can be used in many ways, but a stone out the back is worthless.
- Generally, use side guards if you have the last stone, and keep the centre clear for your last shot. On the other hand, if the opposition has last stone, play centre guards and try to steal by getting a stone onto the button and hidden.
- Aim to keep it simple – if there is a choice of shots always call the easier one. Let the opposition call the big shots.
- In an even game, plan to give your opposition one shot when they have last stone. Play those ends to make sure they only get one shot. If you happen to get something against the head treat it as a bonus.
- If the score is close don't gamble without last stone unless it is the end of the game and you are needing to steal.
- When you have the last stone, know the ice, and your team has draw weight, go for two. The usual way is to gamble on the wings with corner guards. This leaves the way to the four-foot circle clear so that if things go wrong you can draw the last stone to save the end.
- When the game is going against you, for example you are three or more shots down or have to steal at the last end,

you will have to gamble. Draw rather than strike; use any stones in play as guards, or freeze up to shots in the house. On the other hand, if you're well ahead, try to prevent the opposition from piling up shots by keeping the head clear.

Skips acquire knowledge and experience over several seasons. Sometimes, however, a relatively inexperienced player is thrown in at the deep end and he has no option but to do the best he can. The experts have even more on offer for new skips:

- All skips should have a firm idea in their minds and know where they are going.
- Learn the ice as quickly as possible, especially the draw to the tee on both hands.
- Use the ring markings along the tee line in the house as the reference points for giving ice, learning and remembering.
- Give clear instructions so players understand what you want.
- Watch for changes during the game as the pebble comes off or the temperature alters in the building.
- Learn from every shot played and always have an alternative.
- Stand still behind or beside the house when the opposition is delivering, and keep your brush out of their line.
- Play your team to the best of their ability.
  If a player isn't able to strike – ask for back weight.
  If there is a choice of handle – ask which they prefer.
  If a player puts on too much handle – give less ice.
- If your sweepers can, let them judge the weight of stones and sweep until you disagree.
- Crucial shots in most games are the draw shots – if the skip cannot draw to the four-foot circle he is going to lose many games.
- If you've given the wrong ice, pass a message with one of the sweepers to tell the player.
- Frantic signs to indicate that a player was wide or tight can demoralise a team.
- Be decisive and act quickly to keep the game moving – lengthy discussions make a boring game.

- Make the best possible use of every stone – if it is wide or narrow, heavy or light, concentrate to see what you can do with it. Never turn away from a played stone however bad it might be.
- After the game, suggest tactfully to players with problems that they would enjoy their game far more with a little help. Most ice rinks now have qualified instructors available.

The question is often asked: what makes a good skip. There are as many different kinds of skip as there are skips, but they do have a few common characteristics. A skip will have at least some experience and skill, and a truckload of determination. He'll have the will to succeed and the hunger to win. He will be an artist when he plays the perfect draw around a guard, and a ruthless weapon when he strikes. His brain will calculate like a computer and his voice will shout clear and far. Often he'll be a maverick when he has to wriggle out of a very tight spot and a regular Houdini when he escapes from an impossible trap. He will be a leader, a gentleman and a lover of the game, and if he isn't he only needs a little more practice.

As the ends pass the score will quickly reflect the state of play. Never be disheartened at losing a big end even if the opposition suddenly have wide grins, because they might well relax and not notice your comeback until it's too late. Never be complacent when you have just scored a big end, it gives you a cushion but needs defending for all your worth. It is easier for a good team to come from behind than to hold on to a ten-point lead, because it brings the best out of them. Winning teams have a habit of winning for very good reason: they simply never give up.

The rules are usually observed and are seldom queried. In club curling and some bonspiels there won't be umpires about unless it's the manager, and everything is left to the skips to deal with. If a stone is burned inform your skip and he'll do the necessary. If you touch a stationary stone do the same. The skips are in charge – if they're not allowed to be an argument will soon develop, and the opposing skip will start enforcing the rules to the letter at your expense. Stay calm, tell your skip and accept the decision they reach.

It is a fact of life that many people take life too seriously, and so it is too in curling. There is only one answer to it: politeness and courtesy at all times, as in life. If your opposition plays a good shot be ready to acknowledge it; if it is a brilliant shot praise it; if it is an outright fluke which he didn't deserve laugh it off; if your takeout picked up dirt and missed by a mile, walk away and think only of your next shot. If someone plays a less than perfect stone, offer encouragement with caution or let the silence speak. Soon the opposition will do the same and the game will become friendly and enjoyable.

Some games are destined to be awkward. The reason can be anything from poor ice, a depressed opposition, a bull-headed skip or friction between players – it shouldn't happen, yet it does. The game is slow and boring, the sweepers are cold and everyone wants to go home, but the bell has yet to ring. Often on these occasions the skips will wisely agree a score and shake hands, but if they don't the agony has to be endured. In this case concentration and a positive attitude will do wonders, because a good shot or two can inspire both teams and a good game can be the result. The same principle must apply here: never give up. Play your stones as best you can, sweep the others as hard as you can, concentrate and enjoy – you paid good money for the ice, make the best of it.

A good game, on the other hand, has a habit of bringing out the best in both teams and can only get better. Difficult shots become easy, smiles and brotherhood abound, and when the game ends in a draw everyone is happy that the outcome is fair. Except of course for that takeout which the skip missed and should've got to take the seventh end, it would've made all the difference, he never took enough ice and everyone knew he was going to miss before it left his hand..... Forget it, the game is over.

In a good game the noise quickly escalates as some adrenaline is diverted to the lungs. There are no rules against shouting and in a tight game everyone will forgive you for making a noise, after all the poor skip doesn't even know he's doing it. It does however remain a courtesy not to shout the roof down and distract neighbouring players, and for some this takes a little practice.

Pressure is the skip's problem, not yours. You're there to do a job, not to panic, and to enjoy doing it, so you can safely leave the worrying to the skip and try to support him as best you can. Skips have their own individual ways of dealing with pressure and it might not always look like it, but they can cope. You have to play the stone in your hand, as best you can, according to what he wants. You can get fired up, excited, jubilant, but not worried. Beware of excess adrenaline too: after sweeping a stone down the length of the ice the stone you play yourself will go out the back, because of adrenaline. Relax, focus, concentrate, and play only the stone in your hand.

When playing a stone, the player is the first to know whether the stone is on line, heavy or light, or even perfect. It is a good idea, and helpful to the team, to tell the sweepers immediately what you think of your stone, but only if you're sure. If you get it wrong too often they'll become confused and ignore you, suddenly not sweeping when they should or sweeping too much. But if you're sure, even as a sweeper, communicate quickly and effectively. You're not going to be right all the time, but if you're decent about it they'll forgive you. Once the stone is halfway down the ice the skip can see it much better than you can, and the least said will save many an argument. The skip is in charge of everything, even the sweeping, and what he says goes.

Most games will have a blank end, which is when neither team has a stone in the house to score a shot and take the end, after all sixteen stones have been played. A blank end is played again, but not replayed – the next end is played in the opposite direction as if there had been a score. Therefore the player who played his stone first in the blanked end does so again in the following end. In other words, the same team holds last-stone advantage. See pages 34 and 35 for the methods of scoring or indicating a blank end on the board.

As a game nears the final ends there are many teams in a winning position who find ingenious ways of wasting time. One day someone is going to do it to you, if you do it to them. It is not only totally unfair, it is totally against the spirit of the game, and giving your opponents every chance within the rules to beat you is a very decent thing to do. The emphasis must always be on finding ways to keep the game moving, it makes for a better game and helps to keep players warm. On the other hand there is little point in criticising a team for delaying the game to your disadvantage if they are not doing so, because discussion in the house is allowed and so are measures and cleaning stones and/or the ice.

During a game players often need to leave the ice for a few moments. The accepted practice is to choose a moment when you're not imminently needed for sweeping or playing a stone, leave the ice and be quick about it. Polite players will often wait a little for your return before resuming play, which will not be more than a minute or two, and one day you'll be able to do the same for them.

Once in a while a player might be unfortunate enough to slip or lose his balance. *Try* not to touch any stones, or to slap them with your brush. Practise it in your mind to roll slightly to one side as you fall, so that you land on flesh and not bone. Avoid landing on your coccyx or your back, but if you are going to then try and remember to tuck your chin into your chest immediately. Be careful, and extend the same care to everyone else; when they fall, help them up; when you fall, be sure to clear your head and regain your senses before continuing. *Do not continue if you feel dizzy or nauseous – you might have concussion. Really,* there is no need to worry if you respect the ice, but respect it you must. Beginners especially will benefit from wearing padded clothing until they find their feet.

The final end of a tight game is what every curler enjoys most. After some two hours everyone is playing well and the gallery will be in full attendance to study every stone played. They will discuss it, analyse it, play it themselves – curling is fascinating to watch once you know what you are watching, and the best stones are played in the gallery. With a few stones in the house anything can happen and either side can win, and if your skip secures a victory you're on the right side. In games like those there really aren't any losers, because there is no disgrace in having done your best and having done it well. Whichever way it finishes, be ready to shake hands with everyone, spend a few moments to clear and park the stones, check that the score card has been filled in, collect all your gear and go and change your clothing if you need to. Then make your way to the bar for a drink and well-deserved socialising, it is your chance to have all the conversations you didn't have time for on the ice. Remember, winners buy the first round, it's supposed to make the losers feel better.

Important note: if your team ever scores eight shots in a single end of a competition, leave them where they are and find the manager. It is extremely rare and could well have a reward.

When all is done
And you have won,
Don't head straight for your car.
Those defeated
Should be treated,
With a drink up at the bar!

Competitions

The essential purpose of all competitions is to decide a winner, and in the same process a ranking of those who take part. In curling the purpose exists and is applied, but there are inherent problems which an ideal competition does not have to overcome.

Firstly, there is the size of the ice rink, and the number of rinks it can provide. Secondly there is the time factor, restricting the number of games that can be played on each rink during each day. Thirdly there is the number of entries, which often exceed the availability of rinks. Finally, to make matters even worse, no team should play two consecutive games on the same sheet of ice. To overcome these problems several formats have been devised, adapted and mixed, by which a winner can be decided. While every effort is made to provide fairness at every stage, no satisfactory format has yet been found which can be said to be totally fair to all.

The simplest format is the Round Robin. Every team in the competition plays every other team once – or twice – and accumulates points, usually two for a win and one for a draw Should two or more teams end with the same score, and this often happens, there will be a play-off to decide the winner. In club competitions the play-off is usually not required or desirable, because of no real requirement to decide a winner and the club's curling schedule.

The advantages of the Round Robin are numerous. It can be played over a weekend, a week or an entire season. Each team will know in advance who their opposition will be. The ice can be booked in advance and ice rinks know exactly when to prepare the rinks. It is a very fair format of competition, probably the fairest, and the simplest to understand. Following a first stage of various playdowns it is the format used in the second stage of all national competitions, to decide the ranking of qualifiers, and is followed by different formats to decide the ultimate winners.

There are however disadvantages. It does not always produce a clear winner. If there are quite a few teams in a competition of two or three days' duration it can be very difficult to get through all the games, and then still find time for the deciding play-offs. As it often takes place over a long period of time an improving team can suffer at the beginning while only reaching its real potential towards the latter stages, giving an average team a better chance to qualify. It is therefore used as a method of selecting several teams who go through to a different format, usually a knockout system, which eliminates most of the problems.

A ladder format is sometimes used for much the same purpose, where a team can challenge another team above it in ranking and so climb higher. After a given period of time, usually a whole season, the top few teams have a weekend of finals on a different format to decide the winner. This isn't a very popular format because it can be difficult to arrange players and ice at short notice, but it does serve the purpose of allowing improving teams an opportunity to challenge the better teams at the top.

In weekend bonspiels it is essential to produce a winner within the time allotted by the ice rink. The first thing the rink will do is to limit the number of entries according to the ice slots available, say sixteen teams to a four-rink venue over two days. Then teams are allowed to enter at random, or are invited to do so, until the list is full, and ice rinks allow for one or two reserves. But to play a Round Robin between sixteen teams over a weekend is clearly impossible, because no team can curl for some sixteen hours a day even if ice were available, so a different format was devised.

The Schenkel System is a format which solves most of the problems of bonspiels. Based on regular ranking after every round, it allows for a certain number of teams to compete and produce a winner over a short period of time. Typically sixteen teams will enter for the Weekend Bonspiel at a four-sheet ice rink, with four sessions of ice during the daytime or evening, and an interval between the sessions.

Even with a format in place there are variations within the format. It is always wise for everyone to know before going onto the ice exactly which system and variation will be used, and to be sure they understand what it means. The number of ends, points for a win or draw, shots, ends and shots up are all relevant and can all vary, including the order used for ranking, and it is essential for every skip to ensure that he has the correct information.

The position of the scorer must never be underestimated. It is very easy to make a mistake and scorers take great care to produce an accurate sheet to avoid complications. Sometimes awkward decisions have to be made by the umpire or organiser which won't always please everybody, but fortunately curlers are generally appreciative and seldom take serious issue. With increasing use and availability of computers the pencil and paper hieroglyphics will soon be replaced by accurate, readable printouts produced after every round, and mistakes are destined to become few and far between.

The following pages contain the results of a weekend bonspiel with the Schenkel System as the format throughout. First the teams are ranked at random – the organiser uses his knowledge and common sense to ensure that the better and more experienced teams will all have an equal share of competing against poorer teams. The names are written down in list form, the entries are divided into two groups and allocated sheets or rinks as they're listed.

With four rounds over one weekend, it has been decided that ranking will be based on points, shots, ends, and shots up, strictly in that order. After every round the new ranking decides the next order of play, until four rounds are completed and a clear winner produced. Scores have been entered at random with no preference to any team, though in keeping with the problems an organiser will have to resolve as the competition progresses. It is also not a typical score sheet, usually these will contain all the information on one sheet which will be several times larger than these pages allow, or a simpler sheet with less information will be used.

Schenkel Bonspiel — First Round — Saturday Morning

Rank	Team	Time	Rink	Points		Shots		Ends		Shots up		Pts	Sh	Ends	S up	Rank
1	Phil	0900	A		2		9		6		+2	2	9	6	+2	3
2	Pat	0900	A		0		7		4		-2	0	7	4	-2	6
3	Ann	0900	B		0		4		3		-5	0	4	3	-5	8
4	John	0900	B		2		9		7		+5	2	9	7	+5	2
5	Graham	0900	C		2		8		5		+1	2	8	5	+1	4
6	Peter	0900	C		0		7		5		-1	0	7	5	-1	5
7	June	0900	D		2		11		6		+5	2	11	6	+5	1
8	Janet	0900	D		0		6		4		-5	0	6	4	-5	7
1	Chris	1130	A		1		7		6		0	1	7	6	0	4
2	George	1130	A		1		7		4		0	1	7	4	0	5
3	Andrew	1130	B		0		5		3		-7	0	5	3	-7	7
4	Cheryl	1130	B		2		12		7		+7	2	12	7	+7	2
5	Jenny	1130	C		2		14		8		+11	2	14	8	+11	1
6	Adam	1130	C		0		3		2		-11	0	3	2	-11	8
7	Preston	1130	D		2		10		5		+1	2	10	5	+1	3
8	Gail	1130	D		0		9		5		-1	0	9	5	-1	6

Schenkel Bonspiel — Second Round — Saturday Afternoon

Rank	Team	Time	Rink	Points		Shots		Ends		Shots up		Pts	Sh	Ends	S up	Rank
1	June	1400	A	2	2	11	10	6	6	+5	+3	4	21	12	+8	1
2	John	1400	A	2	0	9	7	7	4	+5	-3	2	16	11	+2	3
3	Phil	1400	B	2	0	9	6	6	4	+2	-3	2	15	10	-1	4
4	Graham	1400	B	2	2	8	9	5	5	+1	+3	4	17	10	+4	2
5	Peter	1400	D	0	1	7	8	5	5	-1	0	1	15	10	-1	6
6	Pat	1400	D	0	1	7	8	4	4	-2	0	1	15	8	-2	7
7	Janet	1400	C	0	2	6	8	4	6	-5	+3	2	14	10	-2	5
8	Ann	1400	C	0	0	4	5	3	4	-5	-3	0	9	7	-8	8
1	Jenny	1630	A	2	0	14	6	8	3	+11	-4	2	20	11	+7	4
2	Cheryl	1630	A	2	2	12	10	7	6	+7	+4	4	22	13	+11	1
3	Preston	1630	B	2	0	10	7	5	4	+1	-2	2	17	9	-1	5
4	Chris	1630	B	1	2	7	9	6	6	0	+2	3	16	12	+2	3
5	George	1630	C	1	2	7	12	4	7	0	+6	3	19	11	+6	2
6	Gail	1630	C	0	0	9	6	5	3	-1	-6	0	15	8	-7	7
7	Andrew	1630	D	0	2	5	11	3	6	-7	+3	2	16	9	-4	6
8	Adam	1630	D	0	0	3	8	2	3	-11	-3	0	11	5	-14	8

Schenkel Bonspiel — Third Round — Sunday Morning

Rank	Team	Time	Rink	Points		Shots		Ends		Shots up		Pts	Sh	Ends	S up	Rank
1	June	0900	C	4	0	21	7	12	4	+8	-1	4	28	16	+7	3
2	Graham	0900	C	4	2	17	8	10	4	+4	+1	6	25	14	+5	1
3	John	0900	D	2	1	16	8	11	5	+2	0	3	24	16	+2	4
4	Phil	0900	D	2	1	15	8	10	5	-1	0	3	23	15	-1	5
5	Janet	0900	A	2	2	14	15	10	7	-2	+9	4	29	17	+7	2
6	Peter	0900	A	1	0	15	6	10	3	-1	-9	1	21	13	-10	7
7	Pat	0900	B	1	0	15	6	8	4	-2	-3	1	21	12	-5	8
8	Ann	0900	B	0	2	9	9	7	5	-8	+3	2	18	12	-5	6
1	Cheryl	1130	D	4	0	22	8	13	5	+11	-3	4	30	18	+8	3
2	George	1130	D	3	2	19	11	11	5	+6	+3	5	30	16	+9	1
3	Chris	1130	C	3	2	16	9	12	5	+2	+2	5	25	17	+4	2
4	Jenny	1130	C	2	0	20	7	11	4	+7	-2	2	27	15	+5	5
5	Preston	1130	A	2	0	17	7	9	3	-1	-4	2	24	12	-5	7
6	Andrew	1130	A	2	2	16	11	9	7	-4	+4	4	27	16	0	4
7	Gail	1130	B	0	2	15	12	8	6	-7	-4	2	27	14	-11	6
8	Adam	1130	B	0	0	11	8	5	4	-14	+4	0	19	9	-10	8

Schenkel Bonspiel — Fourth Round — Sunday Afternoon

Rank	Team	Time	Rink	Points		Shots		Ends		Shots up		Pts	Sh	Ends	S up	Rank
1	Graham	1400	B	6	0	25	6	14	4	+7	-3	6	31	18	+4	2
2	Janet	1400	B	4	2	29	9	17	5	+7	+3	6	38	22	+10	1
3	June	1400	A	4	0	28	7	16	3	+7	-4	4	35	19	+4	5
4	John	1400	A	3	2	24	11	16	6	+2	+4	5	35	22	+6	3
5	Phil	1400	C	3	2	23	12	15	7	-1	+6	5	35	22	+5	4
6	Ann	1400	C	2	0	18	6	12	3	-5	-6	2	24	15	-11	7
7	Peter	1400	D	1	2	21	11	13	6	-5	+7	3	32	19	+2	6
8	Pat	1400	D	1	0	21	4	12	3	-5	-7	1	25	15	-12	8
1	George	1630	B	5	0	30	8	16	5	+9	-1	5	38	21	+8	3
2	Chris	1630	B	5	2	25	9	17	5	+4	+1	7	34	22	+5	1
3	Cheryl	1630	C	4	0	30	6	18	3	+8	-4	4	36	21	+4	5
4	Andrew	1630	C	4	2	27	10	16	6	0	+4	6	37	22	+4	2
5	Jenny	1630	A	2	2	27	8	15	6	+5	+3	4	35	21	+8	6
6	Gail	1630	A	2	0	27	5	14	4	-11	-3	2	32	18	-14	7
7	Preston	1630	D	2	2	24	13	12	8	-5	+8	4	37	20	+3	4
8	Adam	1630	D	0	0	19	5	9	2	-10	-8	0	24	11	-18	8

After two days of serious fun the results are listed very simply with the ranking finally achieved. Sometimes there is a final and semi-final between the top four teams, or a play-off to decide the outright winner. If a play-off does take place in this bonspiel, the ranking and rinks are given below.

Schenkel Bonspiel — Final Rankings

Rank	Team	Pts	Sh	Ends	S up	Rink
1	Janet	6	38	22	+10	C
2	Graham	6	31	18	+4	A
3	John	5	35	22	+6	D
4	Phil	5	35	22	+5	B
5	June	4	35	19	+4	-
6	Peter	3	32	19	+2	-
7	Ann	2	24	15	-11	-
8	Pat	1	25	15	-12	-
1	Chris	7	34	22	+5	C
2	Andrew	6	37	22	+4	A
3	George	5	38	21	+8	D
4	Preston	4	37	20	+3	B
5	Cheryl	4	36	21	+4	-
6	Jenny	4	35	21	+8	-
7	Gail	2	32	18	-14	-
8	Adam	0	24	11	-18	-

For this particular competition the duration of each game was ten ends, with no extra ends, and as a result there were some draws where teams received a point each. It is also obvious from the score sheets that ten ends were not always scored in each game, and this is simply because some ends were blanked. Note that all teams played four games.

The preceeding sheets demonstrate what is best described as the true Schenkel system, as it originally was. It has evolved a little, and so has the methods of recording the information, but the sheets are included for curlers to be able to follow the details from game to game along with the changes in ranking.

Counting shots first in the ranking often leads to one team gaining a twenty-shot advantage in an early game, which firstly ruins the losers prospects of a good competition, and secondly gives the winner an unfair advantage over other teams who have had tighter games. The spirit of curling is playing to win, but not to humble your opponents – beating someone by twenty shots is definitely humiliation of a kind. Furthermore, in an effort to keep the scores down many teams will resort to the defensive striking game, so causing many blanked ends.

The change introduced was to count ends before shots, which has now become the accepted norm. Blanked ends are now wasted ends which might be needed later, and a much fairer approach to scoring has been the result. It remains however important to make sure before a competition what the criteria are, a mistake on this matter can be very costly. When ends are counted before shots, a different team can easily be the winner, but in reality teams would play to a different strategy and the better teams would usually have the upper hand anyway.

When the rules require each game to produce a winner with an extra end(s), it would be usual to score one point only for each win, which makes no difference to the outcome. Again, in this example, the outcome might be different for certain teams, while in reality the better teams would cope with it.

As for presenting results during a competition, there are better ways. Organisers and umpires have printed sheets on which they enter details and from which they achieve the ranking for each round. Remember that they often have very little time between rounds to decide rankings and allocate sheets of ice, and only once the next round is underway are they able to bring complicated scoresheets up to date and copied for analysis by the competitors. A simplified scoresheet appears on the next page, using the results after the first round.

Schenkel Bonspiel — Section A — Draw One — Results

Phil	9	—	7	Pat
Ann	4	—	9	John
Graham	8	—	7	Peter
June	11	—	6	Janet

Schenkel Bonspiel — Section A — Draw One — Ranking

Team	Points	Shots	Ends	Shots up
June	2	11	6	+5
John	2	9	7	+5
Phil	2	9	6	+2
Graham	2	8	5	+1
Peter	0	7	5	-1
Pat	0	7	4	-2
Janet	0	6	4	-5
Ann	0	4	3	-5

It goes without saying that the same scoresheet can be used for any competition. It is quick and easy, and the rinks and times can be added to enable the organiser to provide essential information to the competitors before they hurry off for refreshment.

When there is no requirement for all teams to play the same number of games the knockout format can be used, or the format changes at a certain stage to a straight knockout. The knockout system can be a single knockout, where a team is out after one defeat, or a double, after two defeats, or even a triple. The double knockout is the most popular and is increasingly seen as a very fair system for serious competition. The format can also be drawn up in advance, giving teams a fair indication of whom they might play in later rounds. They can also be modified, as the one below has been, to produce a winner. These changes will be written into the "Conditions of Competition", which is issued to all competitors before the start of the event.

Double-Knockout System

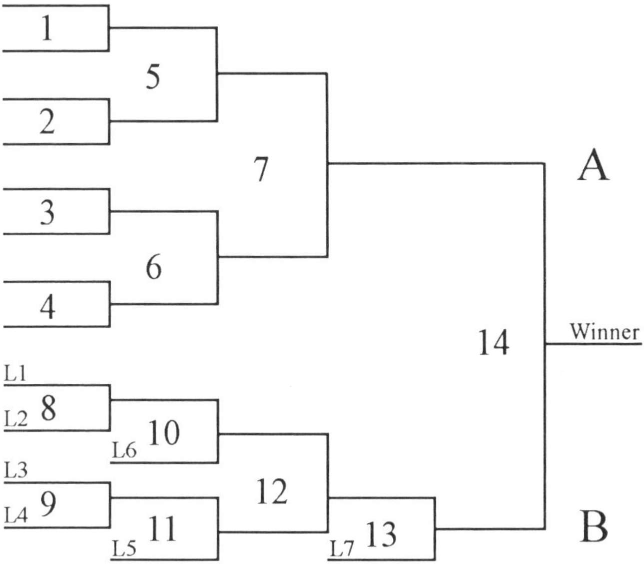

With eight teams starting and all games played to win, after one round there will be four winners with the losers moving to the B Group. Of these only the winners remain, the losers having lost twice. At the end there will remain one winner in Group A who hasn't lost at all, and one in Group B who has only lost once. It is very straightforward and simple, and may the best team win!

On the following pages is another way of using the double-knockout system, with sixteen teams playing a bonspiel.

Weekend Bonspiel — First Round — Saturday Morning

Rank	Team	Time	Rink	Points		Shots		Ends		Shots up		Pts	Sh	Ends	S up	Rank
1	Phil	0900	A		2		9		6		+2	2	9	6	+2	6
2	Pat	0900	A		0		7		4		-2	0	7	4	-2	12
3	Ann	0900	B		0		4		3		-5	0	4	3	-5	15
4	John	0900	B		2		9		7		+5	2	9	7	+5	5
5	Graham	0900	C		2		8		5		+1	2	8	5	+1	7
6	Peter	0900	C		0		7		5		-1	0	7	5	-1	11
7	June	0900	D		2		11		6		+5	2	11	6	+5	3
8	Janet	0900	D		0		6		4		-5	0	6	4	-5	13
9	Chris	1130	A		1		7		6		0	1	7	6	0	8
10	George	1130	A		1		7		4		0	1	7	4	0	9
11	Andrew	1130	B		0		5		3		-7	0	5	3	-7	14
12	Cheryl	1130	B		2		12		7		+7	2	12	7	+7	2
13	Jenny	1130	C		2		14		8		+11	2	14	8	+11	1
14	Adam	1130	C		0		3		2		-11	0	3	2	-11	16
15	Preston	1130	D		2		10		5		+1	2	10	5	+1	4
16	Gail	1130	D		0		9		5		-1	0	9	5	-1	10

Weekend Bonspiel — Second Round — Saturday Afternoon — **Low Road**

1	George	1400	B	1	2	7	10	4	6	0	+4	3	17	10	+4	5
2	Gail	1400	B	0	0	9	6	5	4	-1	-4	0	15	9	-5	-
3	Peter	1400	D	0	0	7	5	5	3	-1	-7	0	12	8	-8	-
4	Pat	1400	D	0	2	7	12	4	6	-2	+7	2	19	10	+5	7
5	Janet	1400	C	0	2	6	9	4	6	-5	+5	2	15	10	0	10
6	Andrew	1400	C	0	0	5	4	3	3	-7	-5	0	9	6	-12	-
7	Ann	1400	A	0	2	4	14	3	8	-5	+11	2	18	11	+6	8
8	Adam	1400	A	0	0	3	3	2	2	-11	-11	0	6	4	-22	-

Weekend Bonspiel — Second Round — Saturday Afternoon — **High Road**

1	Jenny	1630	A	2	2	14	9	8	5	+11	+1	4	23	13	+12	**1**
2	Cheryl	1630	A	2	0	12	8	7	5	+7	-1	2	20	12	+6	6
3	June	1630	B	2	0	11	6	6	4	+5	-3	2	17	10	+2	9
4	Preston	1630	B	2	2	10	9	5	5	+1	+3	4	19	10	+4	**3**
5	John	1630	C	2	2	9	8	7	6	+5	+3	4	17	13	+8	**4**
6	Phil	1630	C	2	0	9	5	6	3	+2	-3	2	14	9	-1	11
7	Graham	1630	D	2	2	8	11	5	7	+1	+5	4	19	12	+6	**2**
8	Chris	1630	D	1	0	7	6	6	3	0	-5	1	13	9	-5	12

Weekend Bonspiel — Third Round — Sunday Morning — **Low Road**

Rank	Team	Time	Rink	Points		Shots		Ends		Shots up		Pts	Sh	Ends	S up	Rank
1	George	0900	C	3	2	17	9	10	5	+4	+2	5	26	15	+6	1
2	Cheryl	0900	C	2	0	20	7	12	4	+6	-2	2	27	16	+4	-
3	Pat	0900	B	2	2	19	8	10	5	+5	+2	4	27	15	+7	2
4	Ann	0900	B	2	0	18	6	11	5	+6	-2	2	24	16	+4	-
5	June	0900	D	2	0	17	6	10	3	+2	-4	2	23	13	-2	-
6	Janet	0900	D	2	2	15	10	10	7	0	+4	4	25	17	+4	3
7	Phil	0900	A	2	1	14	9	9	5	-1	0	3	23	14	-1	4
8	Chris	0900	A	1	1	13	9	9	5	-5	0	2	22	14	-5	-

Weekend Bonspiel — Third Round — Sunday Morning — **High Road**

Rank	Team	Time	Rink	Points		Shots		Ends		Shots up		Pts	Sh	Ends	S up	Rank
1	Jenny	1130	B	4	0	23	6	13	4	+12	-1	4	29	17	+11	**3**
2	Graham	1130	B	4	2	19	7	12	4	+6	+1	6	26	16	+7	**2**
3	Preston	1130	D	4	2	19	9	10	5	+4	+1	6	28	15	+5	**1**
4	John	1130	D	4	0	17	8	13	4	+8	-1	4	25	17	+7	**4**

Weekend Bonspiel — Finals — Sunday Afternoon — **Low Road**

Rank	Team	Time	Rink	Points		Shots		Ends		Shots up		Pts	Sh	Ends	S up	Rank
1	George	1500	B	5	2	26	9	15	5	+6	+4	7	35	20	+10	W
2	Pat	1500	B	4	0	27	5	15	5	+7	-4	4	32	20	+3	R
3	Janet	1500	D	4	2	25	8	17	6	+4	+2	6	33	23	+6	3
4	Phil	1500	D	3	0	23	6	14	4	-1	-2	3	29	18	-3	4

Low Road: Winner — George
Runner-up — Pat

Weekend Bonspiel — Finals — Sunday Afternoon — **High Road**

Rank	Team	Time	Rink	Points		Shots		Ends		Shots up		Pts	Sh	Ends	S up	Rank
1	Preston	1500	C	6	0	28	6	15	4	+5	-3	6	34	19	+2	**R**
2	Graham	1500	C	6	2	26	9	16	5	+7	+3	8	35	21	+10	**W**
3	Jenny	1500	A	4	0	29	7	17	4	+11	-3	4	36	21	+8	**3**
4	John	1500	A	4	2	25	10	17	6	+7	+3	6	35	23	+10	**4**

High Road: Winner — Graham
Runner-up — Preston

The double-knockout system with a High Road and a Low Road is the one curlers are most likely to come across in weekend bonspiels. After the first round, which takes place exactly the same as another knockout, only winners remain in the High Road. Teams who lose a second time also fall out of the Low Road, while losers in the High Road move to the Low Road for their next game. It is a popular format which allows losers more games then they would otherwise have had.

There is of course no real difference between this layout and the one on page 97, except for the final game, but there is no need in weekend bonspiels to be clinical about the finish. Good curling, and lots of it, is really what weekends are all about, and the socialising will more than compensate for the loss of two games.

The simplest format is of course a straight knockout, where the winners keep playing each other until only one team remains. Simple it might be, but the first ranking is often down to luck and most teams will only get two games. It does however allow a large number of teams to enter a competition and soon reduces the number to manageable proportions.

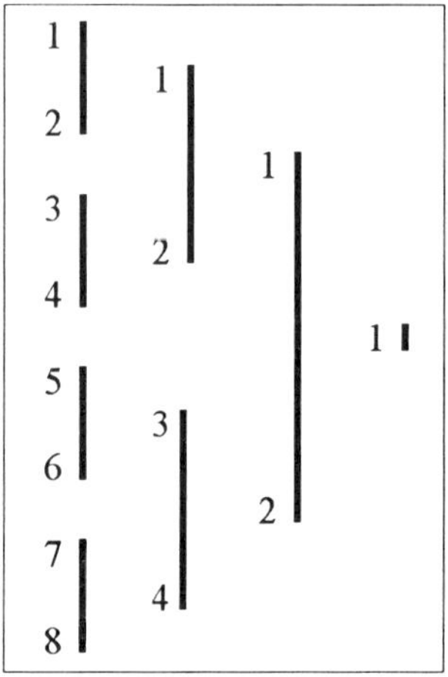

Points

Usually most clubs will hold an annual event of Points Competition. They will use at least two rinks alongside each other and often four, playing first in one direction and then return along the next rink in the other. This ensures that many exercises are played both on in-turn and out-turn. The sequence of play is often drawn out a hat with the previous year's winner going first, and scores are kept as play progresses. Out of a possible eighty points forty or more is a very good score, with the best players achieving over fifty.

Points can be considered the only part of curling where players are on their own, and it does provide a reasonable assessment of a player's ability to deliver stones accurately. What makes points particularly difficult is the absence of sweepers or a skip in the house. While sweeping of a stone by its own player is often allowed it isn't always practical, and to save time it is usually only allowed on the second of a pair of stones.

Positions of circles to be drawn on the ice

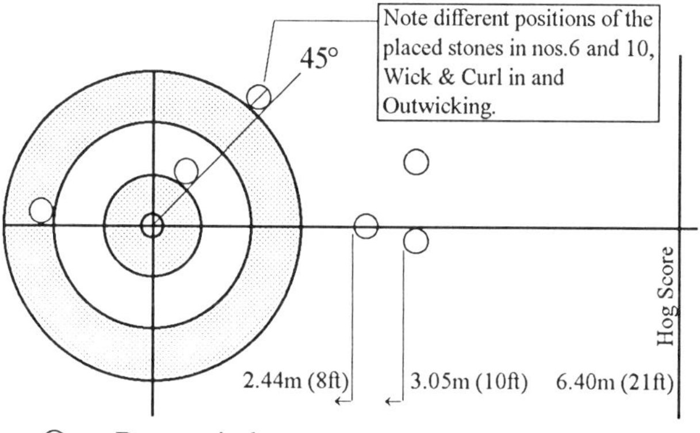

The Rules of Points

(a) Competitors shall draw lots for the rotation of play, and shall use two Stones.

(b) The measurement of the Rink for points play shall be in conformity with the provisions of The Rules.

(c) Two Circles, one having a radius of 1.22m (4ft) and the other having a radius of 1.83m (6ft) shall be drawn round each Tee, and a line through the centre of each Circle from Foot Line to the Hog Line.

(d) Every competitor shall play four shots at each of the nine following points of the game: (1) Striking, (2) Inwicking, (3) Drawing, (4) Guarding, (5) Chap and Lie, (6) Wick and Curl in, (7) Raising, (8) Chipping the Winner, and (9) Drawing through a Port, according to the definitions and diagrams given.

(e) In Nos. (2), (6), (8) and (9), and at (10) Outwicking when played, the object Stones shall be placed so that two shots shall be played on the right at one end and two on the left at the other end.

(f) No Stone shall be considered outside a Circle unless it be entirely clear of that Circle.

(g) In the event of two or more competitors being equal, they shall play four shots at (10) Outwicking. If the competition be still undecided, the Umpire shall order that one or more of the preceding points be played again by the competitors who are equal.

Note: Much time will be saved if two Rinks be prepared lying parallel to each other, the Tee of the one being at the reverse end of the other Rink; every competitor plays both Stones up one Rink and afterwards both down the other, thus finishing at each round all his chances at that point.

● - Placed stones ○ - Played stones

1. Striking

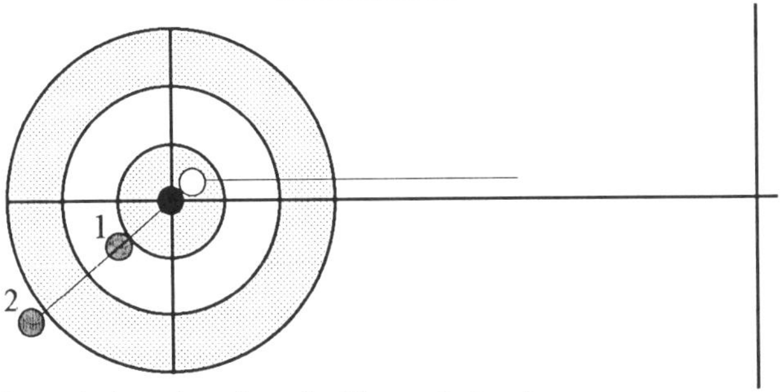

A Stone being placed on the Tee and struck.
If struck, count one.
If struck out of the outer circle, count two.

2. Inwicking

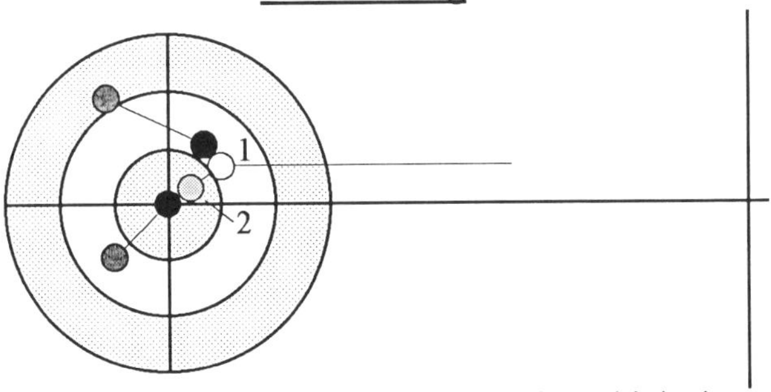

A Stone being placed on the Tee, and another with its inner edge 76cm (2'6") from the Tee, and its fore edge on a line drawn from the Tee at an angle of 45° with the centre line.
If the played stone strikes the latter on the inside, count one.
If it perceptively moves both stones, count two.

3. Drawing

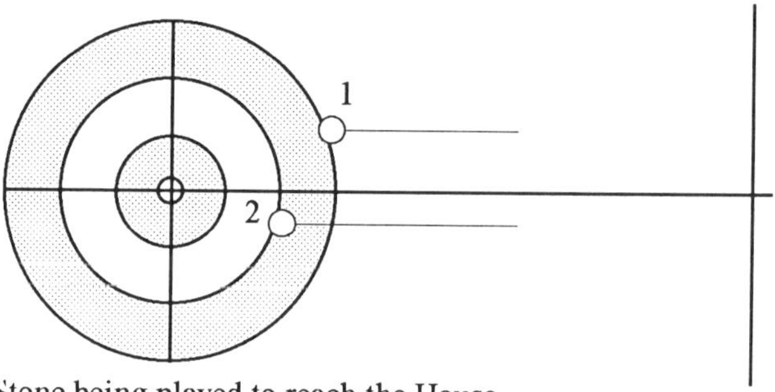

A Stone being played to reach the House.
If it lies within or on the outer circle, count one.
If it lies within or on the 1.22m (4ft) circle, count two.

4. Guarding

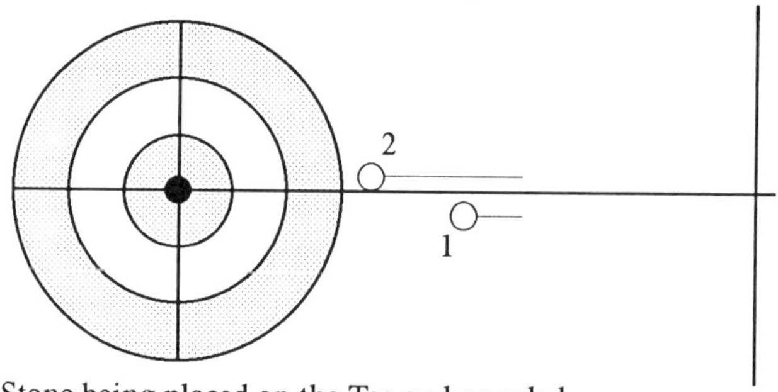

A Stone being placed on the Tee and guarded.
The played Stone must be over the Hog, but must not touch the placed Stone.
If the played Stone comes to rest within 15cm (6in) of the centre line, count one.
If the played Stone comes to rest touching the centre line, count two.

5. Chap and Lie

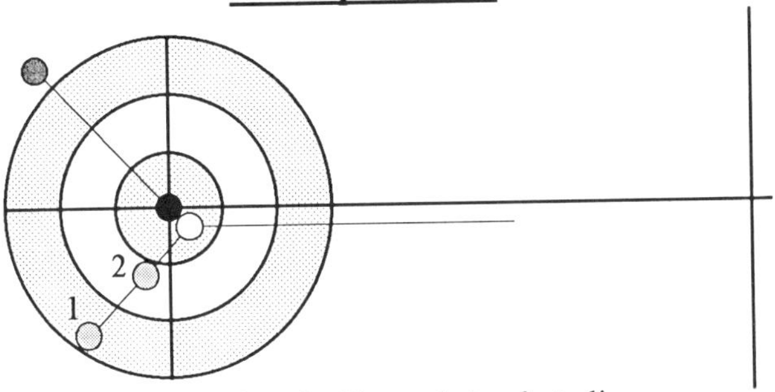

A Stone being placed on the Tee and struck, to lie.
If struck out of the outer circle and the played Stone lies within or on the outer circle, count one.
If struck out of the outer circle and the played Stone lies within or on the 1.22m (4ft) circle, count two.

6. Wick and Curl in.

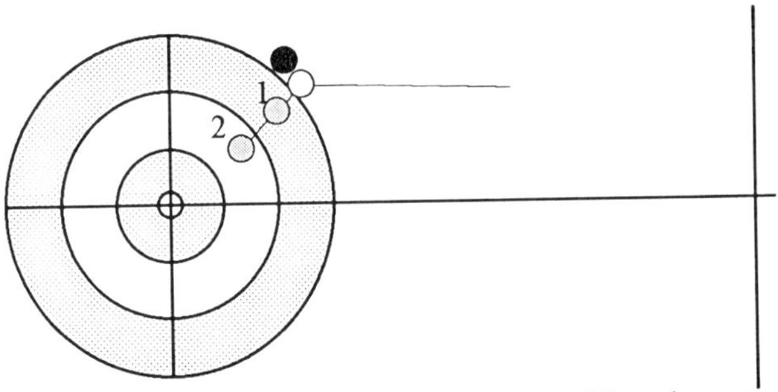

A Stone being placed with its inner edge touching the outer circle, and its **front edge** on a line at an angle of 45° with the centre line and struck, to curl in.
If it struck and the played Stone lies within or on the outer circle, count one.
If it struck and the played Stone lies within or on the 1.22m (4ft) circle, count two.

7. Raising

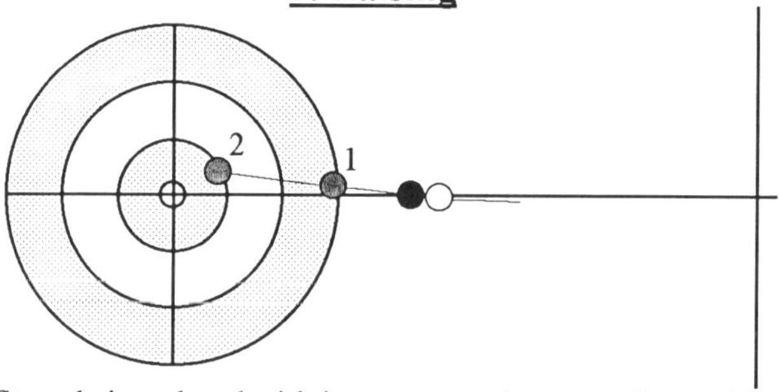

A Stone being placed with its centre on the centre line and its edge 2.44m (8ft) from the Tee, and raised.

If raised to lie on or within the outer circle, count one.
If raised to lie on or within the 1.22m (4ft) circle, count two.

8. Chipping the Winner

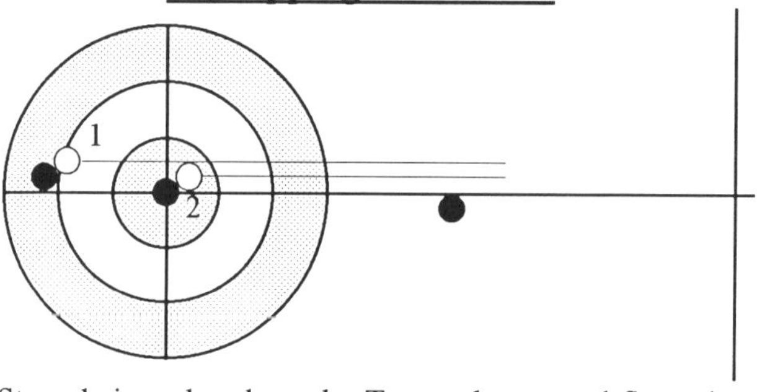

A Stone being placed on the Tee, and a second Stone just touching the centre line with its edge 3.05m (10ft) from the Tee to half-guard it, and a third Stone just touching the centre line but 1.22m (4ft) behind the Tee on the opposite side to the guard, either of the two rear Stones to be chipped.

If the played Stone strikes the Stone behind the Tee, count one.
If the played Stone strikes the Stone on the Tee, count two.
The maximum score for any one Shot is two.

9. Drawing through a Port

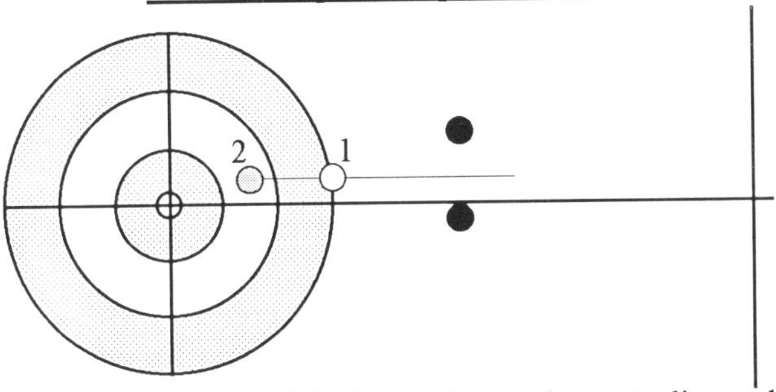

A Stone being placed with its inner edge on the centre line and its edge 3.05m (10ft) from the Tee, and another Stone on the opposite side with its inner edge 0.61m (2ft) from the centre line, to draw the port without touching either Stone.
If the played Stone passes through the port to lie on or within the outer circle, count one.
If the played Stone passes through the port to lie on or within the 1.22m (4ft) circle, count two.

10. Outwicking

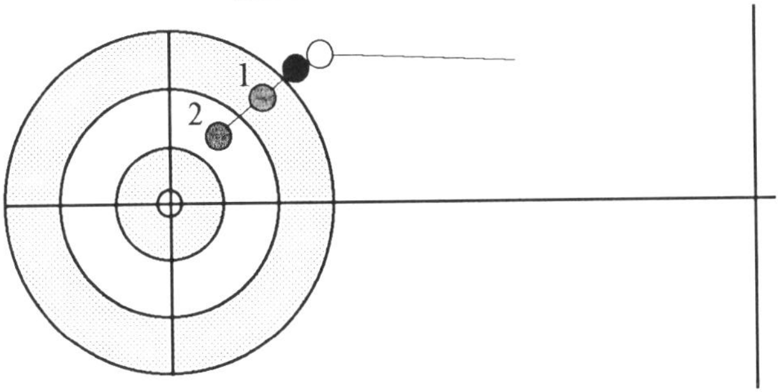

A Stone being placed with its inner edge touching the outer circle and its **centre** on a line at an angle of 45° to be wicked.
If struck to lie on or within the outer circle, count one.
If struck to lie on or within the 3.22m (4ft) circle, count two.

Pairs

Pairs competition in clubs have a similar value to the Points game, in allowing a club to have a very enjoyable day or evening of curling against each other. Typically eight teams of two will compete on a knockout basis, with a High Road and Low Road after the first round.

In serious competitions six ends are played in each round with seven ends in the finals, but clubs often reduce these numbers by one or two to save time. The lead plays his four stones first, alternating with his opponent, and the skips then play four stones each. There is no requirement for the skip (or the lead when the skip plays) to stand in the house, though they usually do.

A game of pairs can often develop into a fine display of touch and accuracy, more so than in normal teamplay. On the whole a draw has a higher percentage of possible success than a strike, especially once there are a few stones in the house. A good team will relish the opportunity to put a stone on the button and guard it for all its worth, and precise play can achieve this. Even in club curling pairs will quickly bring out the best in all players with its intimacy and with the extra stones each player has to find his length.

The value of pairs is easily underestimated in practice. When only four players can make it for a practice session pairs is an ideal way of spending time on the ice, and the format can be readily adapted to three or even two players. With regret not many ice rinks provide opportunities for a pairs bonspiel, it would be welcomed by many curlers.

Curling Rules

Inevitably all games have rules, and many of them are either ignored or flouted. Fortunately the gamesmanship of curling is such that, although the rules do exist, disputes are often settled between the skips. If both skips agree on the original position of a stone accidentally moved there is no problem, and if they can't agree a solution can soon be found with or without the rules.

It is important even at club or social level to be familiar with the rules, and in particular with the more basic ones. For those advancing to more serious competition in leagues and upwards full knowledge of the rules becomes essential. In curling as a sport there will now appear qualified men and women in very warm clothing who act as umpires and will certainly enforce the rules, though the Chief Umpire will still apply common sense and allow the skips to settle their own disputes where possible.

Then there are differences. The Canadians do it one way and the Scots another, some are sticklers and some are not. The World Curling Federation has a rule book and so has the Royal Caledonian Curling Club, and some of the rules differ. But rarely will these differences matter to the average curler and perhaps they're better left to the umpires to study, otherwise the rules will become so many that there will be no room left for a good game of curling.

It is important in this respect to remember that the rules of the RCCC are the rules of the game of curling, while the WCF rules are the rules of international competition. The differences simply will not be a problem. As for differences between various countries, they are so few that there is little point in trying to learn them until it becomes necessary.

The following pages contain the rules of the RCCC, almost exclusively used in Scotland, and very few changes have been made to the original text.

These Rules are reproduced with the permission
of The Royal Caledonian Curling Club
(Revised August 1998)

Words indicating the masculine gender include the feminine gender.

SECTION A - THE RINK

1. The length of the playing area shall be 42.06m (138ft), and where possible the ice should be continued a further 1.22m (4ft) or more behind each foot line. It is recommended that, where possible, the width of the playing area shall be a minimum of 4.75m (15ft 7in).
2. The length of the rink from the foot line to the tee shall be 38.4m (126ft), subject to Section J1(b) & 1(c).
3. The tees shall be 34.75m (114ft) apart and, with the tees as centres, circles having radii of 1.22m (4ft) and 1.83m (6ft) shall be drawn. Additional inner circles may also be drawn. Dividing lines must be drawn from back line to back line or barriers placed between adjoining rinks.
4. A line to be called the centre line shall be drawn from foot line to foot line and through each tee. The foot line, to be 45.72cm (18in) in length, shall be drawn at right angles, on which at 7.62cm (3in) from the centre line, the inside edge of the hack shall be placed.
   Other lines shall be drawn across the rink at right angles to the centre line, and from dividing line to dividing line, as in the diagram, viz:

   (a) A hog line, distant from each tee, one-sixth part of the distance between the foot line and the further tee.
   (b) A tee line through each tee.
   (c) A back line, the back edge of which shall be at a tangent to the six-foot circle at the point where the centre line crosses the back line.
5. All lines shall be as in the accompanying diagram on the following page (*not included here, see page 39*), which shall form part of the Rules subject to Section J1.

SECTION B - THE CURLING STONE

Shape, Weight and Dimensions of the Stone

1. (a) Curling Stones shall be of a circular shape on plan.
   (b) No stone, including its handle and bolt, shall be of greater weight than 19.96kg (44lbs), or of greater circumference than 91.44cm (36 inches), or of less height than 11.43cm (4.5in).

Substitution and Breaking of Stone

2. (a) After a game has started no stone shall be substituted for another except under Section B2(b) or Section C5.
   (b) If a stone is broken in play a replacement stone shall be placed where the largest fragment came to rest. The end in play, and the game, shall be completed using the replacement stone.

Stone Rolling Over, Handle Quitting

3. (a) Any stone which rolls over in its course, or comes to rest on its side or top, shall be removed from play immediately.
   (b) Where the handle of a stone quits the stone in delivery, the player is entitled to replay the stone.

SECTION C - DELIVERY OF STONE

1. Left-handed players shall play from the hack placed on the right-hand side of the centre line and right-handed players shall play from the hack placed on the left-hand side of the centre line.

Delivery from Wrong Hack

2. (a) A stone delivered from the wrong hack should, if possible, be stopped in its progress and removed from the ice.

(b) However, if the stone so played has come to rest or has struck another stone, the played stone shall be removed from play and the displaced stone or stones be placed as nearly as possible where they originally were, to the satisfaction of the opposing skip. Both skips should agree upon the position, but failing agreement, the umpire shall decide.

Release of Stone

3. (a) In the delivery of the stone, the stone shall be clearly seen to be released from the hand before the stone reaches the nearer hog line.

(b) If the player fails so to release the stone, it shall be removed from play immediately by the playing team. If the stone has struck another stone, the played stone shall be removed from play by the playing team and any displaced stone shall be placed as nearly as possible to where it originally lay to the satisfaction of the opposing skip. Benefit to either team is not a factor.

Holding Stone, Returning for Another Delivery

4. No player may hold his stone and return to the hack for another delivery if the stone has reached the nearer tee line, in which event the stone shall be removed from play by the playing side.

Playing Wrong Stone

5. Should a player play a wrong stone, a stone belonging to his team shall be put in its place.

Playing Out of Turn

6. (a) If a player should play out of turn in his team, the stone so played should, if possible, be stopped in its progress and returned to the player.

(b) Should the mistake not be discovered until after the stone has come to rest or has struck another stone, the end shall be continued, as if it had been played properly from the beginning, but the missed stone shall be played by the player missing his turn as the last stone for his side for that end.

(c) Where the skips agree that a stone has been missed but are unable to agree as to which player missed his turn, the lead of the team which made the mistake, shall play the last stone for his team, at that end.

(d) Where two stones of a team are delivered in succession at the same end, the opposite skip shall remove the stone played by mistake, replace to his satisfaction any stone displaced by the stone played by mistake and continue the end as if the mistake had not occurred, and the player who delivered the stone played by mistake shall redeliver it as the last stone for his team at that end.

(e) Where a player delivers three stones at one end, the end shall be continued as if the mistake had not occurred and the fourth player of his team shall deliver only one stone at that end.

Wrongful Delivery

7. No player shall deliver a stone, until the stone delivered by the previous player has come to rest or until such time as any stone whose movement has been generated by that stone comes to rest. In case of infringement, the stone shall be returned to the offending player who shall deliver it correctly.

Stone Not Clearing the Hog Line

8. A stone which does not clear the further hog line shall be a hog and shall be removed from play immediately except where it has struck another stone lying in play.

Stone Crossing Back Line

9. A stone having crossed the back line, and lying clear of it, shall be removed from play immediately.

Stone Touching Sides of Rink

10. Any stone which in its progress touches barriers on either side of the rink shall be removed from play immediately. But, if a stone crosses a dividing line drawn on the ice between rinks, or sheets, and returns to finish within the rink clear of the dividing line, it shall remain in play provided it has not touched any object in the adjoining rink. However, see also Section D2(b).

Running Stone Touched

11. (a) If a running stone is touched by any of the playing team or by his equipment, the touched stone shall be considered burned and be removed from play immediately by that team. However, if in the opinion of the opposing skip, removal of the stone would be beneficial to the offending team, then he may replace the stone as nearly as possible to the position he considers it would have come to rest had it not been touched. He may also reposition any stone or stones that would have been displaced had the running stone not been touched and been allowed to continue. For an opposing skip to reposition any potentially displaced stone(s), the infraction must have occurred inside the hog line at the playing end.

(b) If a running stone is touched by any of the opposing team or by his equipment, the stone shall be placed where the skip of the team to which it belongs considers it would have come to rest if it had not been touched.

(c) If the position of any stone is altered by a touched stone, the skip opposed to the team at fault may elect:

(i) to remove the touched stone and replace all other altered stones to the position where he considers they originally lay; or

(ii) to leave the touched stone and all altered stones where they came to rest.

Displaced Stationary Stones

12. (a) If a stationary stone which would have affected the course of a running stone is displaced by the playing team, the running stone shall be removed from play and any affected stone shall be placed as nearly as possible where the opposing skip considers it originally lay.

(b) If a stationary stone which would have affected the course of a running stone is displaced by the opposing team, the skip of the playing team shall replace any affected stone as nearly as possible where he considers it originally lay or would have come to rest.

(c) If displaced other than stated in (a) and (b) of this Rule, both skips should agree on the positions to which the stones are to be returned.

SECTION D - THE GAME

1. (a) All games shall be:

(i) of a certain number of ends, or

(ii) by time as may be agreed on, or as fixed by the umpire at the outset.

(b) When a game is being played by time, no end shall be started after the finishing time signal has been given, except where extra ends are required.

(c) If the time signal has not been given when the last stone of the last played end has come to rest, then another end shall be played. (The intention of this rule is that another end will not be started if, when the time signal is given, the stone delivered by the previous player has not come to rest or any stone(s) whose movement has been generated by that stone has not come to rest).

Scoring

2. (a) Games shall be decided by a majority of shots. A team

shall score one shot for every stone which is nearer the tee than any stone of the opposing team.

(b) Every stone which is not clearly outside the outer circle shall be eligible to count, even if touching a dividing line.

(c) In the event of the scores being equal at the end of a game play may be continued for one or more ends, as may be agreed on, or as provided for by the conditions of the game or match, or as may be fixed by the umpire.

(d) An end is decided when the skips, or acting skips, in charge of the house at the time agree upon the score for that end.

Measuring

3. (a) No stone shall be measured by instrument until the last stone of the end has come to rest except by the umpire when requested by a skip to decide whether or not a stone is in play or in the free guard zone.

(b) Measurements shall be taken from the tee to the nearest part of the stone.

(c) If two or more stones are so close to the tee that it is impossible to use a measuring device to determine the scoring stone, the determination shall be made visually by the chief umpire. If no decision can be made the end shall be scored as a blank end.

Teams

4. (a) Every team shall be composed of four players, each playing two stones, and playing each stone alternately with his opponent.

(b) Any team not having its full complement of four players shall be subject to Rule 5 of Royal Club Competitions (General Rules and Conditions - Failure to Appear).

(c) When in a competition, owing to illness, accident or any other valid reason, a player is unable to play in any round, he may be replaced by another player as substitute, provided this substitute has not already taken part in that competition in any other team. A substitute may play in any position in any round but not higher than the position of the curler he is replacing. The skip shall declare any substitute in the first round of a competition or the team in the first round will be understood to be the entered team. No team shall take into play more than two substitutes, in any game, match or competition. All substitutes must be eligible in terms of the rules of the competition.

(d) Where a player is unable to continue the skip may:

(i) finish the game then in progress with the remaining players, in which case the first two players shall throw three stones each, or

(ii) bring in a qualified substitute for the game then in progress at the beginning of the next end.

Any substitute must play in the position of the replaced player when entering a game in progress.

(e) A player who has left a game because of illness, accident or other extenuating circumstance may rejoin his team at any time during that game in the competition. If a substitute joins that game, the original player may rejoin his team for the next game.

(f) The teams opposing each other shall settle by lot which side shall lead at the first end, after which the winners of the preceding end shall lead, and shall continue to do so if any extra ends be played.

(g) The rotation of play observed during the first end of a game shall not be changed.

(h) In circumstances not otherwise covered the Royal Club may modify the above Rules to meet with requirements of a specific competition.

The Skip and the Players

5. (a)(i) The skip has the exclusive direction of the game for his team, and may play in any position he pleases in the game, subject to Section D4(g).

(ii) Only skips. or acting skips, are entitled to stand within or behind the house. The skip of the playing side has the choice of place, and he shall not be obstructed by the other skip.

(iii) When his turn to play comes, he shall select one of his players as acting skip.

(iv) The skip may, however, return to the house for brief consultation.

(b)(i) The players other than the skip or acting skip shall not stand behind the house, but shall place themselves along the side of the rink between the hog lines, except when sweeping or about to deliver a stone.

(ii) No player shall cross the rink when a player is about to play; or in front of a stone which is in motion.

SECTION E - SWEEPING

1. The sweeping shall be under the direction of the skips.
2. Any stone in motion is a running stone and only a running stone may be swept.
3. (a) The sweeping motion, which shall be from side to side, shall leave no debris in front of the running stone and shall finish to either side of the stone.

   (b) The sweepers and their equipment must be seen to be clear of the stone at all times.

   Penalty: If a team infringes this rule and the stone involved is their own it shall be removed from play at the discretion of the umpire. However, if the stone involved belongs to the opposition the umpire shall direct the repositioning of the stone to where he considers it would have come to rest had it not been infringed. If in the opinion of the non-offending skip repositioning of the stone would benefit the offending team, it may be left where it came to rest.
4. (a) The player's side may sweep the ice from tee line to tee line but any stone set in motion may only be swept by the side to which it belongs, except behind the tee line, where both skips have an equal right to sweep.

4. (a) The player's side may sweep the ice from tee line to tee line but any stone set in motion may only be swept by the side to which it belongs, except behind the tee line, where both skips have an equal right to sweep.
   (b) Only the player in charge of the head shall be allowed to sweep behind the tee line and shall not start to sweep an opposing stone until the stone reaches the line.
5. At the start of each game, each player shall decide which brush or broom he will use for sweeping purposes during the game and only that brush or broom may be used for sweeping by the player during the game. If the brush or broom becomes unfit for further use during the game it shall be replaced by the same type of brush or broom. The replacement shall be inspected and approved by an umpire prior to use. Brushes may be exchanged between players on the same team during the course of a game but a corn broom may not be exchanged.

SECTION F - THE UMPIRE

1. A suitably qualified umpire may be appointed for any game, match or competition. He shall be a member of the Royal Club and shall be acquainted with these Rules.
2. The duties and powers of an umpire shall be the general supervision of a game, match or competition, the power of settling disputed shots, the enforcement of these rules and the resolution of other problems that may arise in course of play.
3. He may depute another suitable umpire to act in his stead.
4. His decision in respect of all questions affecting the game, match or competition shall be final.
5. He shall satisfy himself that all players are eligible to play.

SECTION G - THE CHIEF UMPIRE

1. A suitably qualified chief umpire who shall be a member of the Royal Club may be appointed for any game, match or competition where the Royal Club Council considers this necessary.
2. Where a chief umpire has been appointed he may intervene in any game at any time and give such directions concerning the conduct of the game as he considers proper.
3. The chief umpire shall ensure prior to any game, match or competition where he has been appointed that the venue satisfies the Royal Club's predetermined conditions.
4. There shall be no appeal against the decision of the chief umpire.
5. In the case of a dispute where the situation is not covered by an existing rule the chief umpire shall make a decision in equity.

SECTION H - FREE GUARD ZONE

The Free Guard Zone will apply for any game, match or competition played under Royal Club Rules excepting the Grand Match and the Points Competition.

1. The area between the hog line and the tee line, excluding the house, shall be a "Free Guard Zone".
2. No stone lying within this zone may be removed from play by the opposition until the first four stones played in any end have come to rest. Any shot played in those circumstances which results in an opposition stone being moved from the free guard zone, either directly or indirectly, to an out of play position is an infraction which shall result in the played stone being removed from play and any other stone if moved being replaced where it previously lay. All stones shall be replaced to the satisfaction of the skip of the non-offending team.

3. For any stone lying in the house, the normal Rules of Play shall apply at all times. A stone may be measured by instrument by an umpire to determine whether or not it is in the house.
4. In all other respects the normal Rules of Play shall apply.

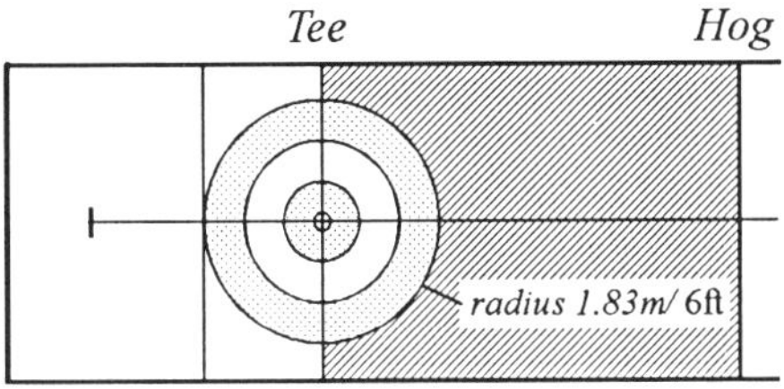

The Free Guard Zone

SECTION I - ETIQUETTE

Curling is a game of skill and of traditions. A shot well played is a delight to see, as is a game played in the true spirit of curling. Curlers play to win but never to humble their opponents. Curling has always relied on the common sense, the honesty and the good manners of the players and a sporting approach to the game. This spirit should influence both the interpretation and application of the rules of the game and also the conduct of all participants both on and off the ice.

SECTION J - THE OUTDOOR GAME

1. (a) Players shall play from the hack or crampit. When hack and crampit are both being used in the same rink, the heel of the crampit will be placed on the foot line and the hack. if used, placed immediately in front of the crampit.

(b) If from any change of weather after a game has begun, or from any other reasonable cause, one side should desire to shorten the rink, or to change to another, and if the two skips cannot agree, the umpire shall, after seeing one end played, determine whether and by how much the rink shall be shortened, or whether it shall be changed, and his decision shall be final.

(c) In no case, however, shall the rink be shortened to less than 29.26m (96ft) from the foot line to the tee.

(d) Should there be no umpire, or should he be otherwise engaged, the two skips may call in any neutral curler to decide, and his powers shall be equal with those of an umpire.

Stopping, Postponing a Game

2. (a) Should the skips not agree, the umpire shall, in the event of the ice appearing to him to be dangerous, stop the game.

(b) He shall postpone the game, even if begun, when the state of the ice is, in his opinion, not fitted for testing the curling skill of the players.

(c) Except in very special circumstances, of which the umpire shall be judge, the game or match shall not proceed, or be continued:

(i) when a thaw has fairly set in;

(ii) when snow is falling and likely to continue during the game or match, or

(iii) if darkness comes on to prevent the played stones being well seen by players at the other end of the rink.

(d) In every case of such postponement to another day the game or match, when renewed, must begin anew.

Cleaning Rink

3. (a) At the completion of any end, either of the skips may call upon all the players to clean and sweep the entire rink.

(b) If objected to, this shall be subject to the approval of the umpire.

Sweeping

4. When snow is falling or drifting, both skips have equal right to clean and sweep the ice behind the tee line.

Reversing of Stone

5. During a game, the sole of a stone may be reversed provided the player be ready when his turn comes.

ROYAL CLUB COMPETITIONS

GENERAL RULES AND CONDITIONS

Definitions

1. (a) *Game*: Play between two teams by time or a given number of ends.
   (b) *Match*: A contest of two or more teams playing against an equal number of teams.
   (c) *Competition*: A playdown by any number of teams playing games or matches to determine a final winner.

Composition of Team

2. (a) A team shall only comprise of members whose subscription to the Royal Club has been paid for the current season.
   (b) It shall be the Skip's responsibility at the date of entry to name the team and to inform the Royal Club in writing of any subsequent changes which might affect the entry. A player so nominated shall be ineligible to play for any other team in that competition except with the written consent of the Royal Club.
   After play has commenced in a competition changes in the composition of a team shall be in accordance with Rule 3.

(c) A team may be entered for a Royal Club competition at only one affiliated Ice Rink.

Substitution

3. (a) Any substitution shall be in accordance with Section D – The Game 4 (c), (d) and (e) and notwithstanding shall be referred to and approved by the Chief Umpire.

(b) A player who has left a game because of illness, accident or other extenuating circumstance may rejoin his team at any time during any game in the competition. If a substitute joins that game the original player may only rejoin his team for the next game.

Conduct of Games

4. (a) Unless individual competition rules state otherwise all games shall be 10 ends but not exceeding the session times as prescribed by the Ice Rink.
In District Playdowns and Finals 10-end games shall be played except as provided in 5(b).

(b) In the event of a tie in a game where a result/winner is necessary an extra end shall be played as required.

(c) A team may concede only after consultation with the Chief Umpire.

Failure to Appear

5. (a)(i) A team entered to play with a member(s) failing to appear on the ice after five minutes of the starting signal shall forfeit one shot, and one shot for each additional five minutes up to a maximum of 30 minutes when the offending team shall forfeit the game.
No dispensation to this rule shall be granted for any reason whatsoever.

(ii) Where the competition rules specify a game to be a number of ends with ends scored as a method of deciding the result or ranking a team with a member(s) failing to appear on the ice shall be penalised, depending on the length of time, as follows:

5 mins	0 ends	+	1 shot
10 mins	1 end	+	2 shots
15 mins	1 end	+	3 shots
20 mins	2 ends	+	4 shots
25 mins	3 ends	+	5 shots
30 mins	game forfeited.		

Where a late penalty applies in any game, ends forfeited shall be deducted from the total ends to be played.

(b) Upon forfeiture of the game the following penalties shall be imposed:

(i) Six shots shall be awarded to the non-offending team and also deducted from the offending team.

(ii) Games played to session times:

Under 1 hr 40 mins	4 ends awarded
1 hr 40 mins and over but under 2 hrs I0 mins	5 ends awarded
2 hrs 10 mins and over	6 ends awarded

No ends shall be awarded to the offending team.

(iii) Games played to a fixed number of ends:

6-7 ends	4 ends awarded
8-9 ends	5 ends awarded
10 ends	6 ends awarded

(c) The latecomers rule shall apply whether games are played by time or a fixed number of ends; if by a fixed number of ends the penalty shall be applied and the game shall be played to a session time as determined by the Umpire.

(d) A team entered to play and failing to appear at a competition and not giving notice in writing to reach the Secretary of the Royal Club not less than two weeks prior to the start of the competition shall be liable for the payment of ice charges arising from the default.

A full copy of the RCCC Rules and Competitions is available from their office. Please contact:

The Secretary
The Royal Caledonian Curling Club
Cairnie House
Ingliston Showground
Newbridge
Midlothian
EH28 2NB
Scotland

Phone 0131-333 3003
Fax 0131-333 3323

The rules of the WCF have specific relevance to international competition. For a copy please contact:

Secretariat
The World Curling Federation
81 Great King Street
Edinburgh
EH3 6RN
Scotland

Phone 0131-5564884
Fax 0131-5569400

The Future

Curling, as a game played by all generations for hundreds of years, has evolved into a modern activity within the comforts of a modern ice rink. Its players have evolved into very skilful curlers, though it could be argued that their skills might not be any better or worse than fifty years ago. Although North America might have ten times more curlers than Europe, it also does not follow that they can curl ten times better. This is perhaps the essence of curling, where its value as a game is judged not purely by excellence, but by the fun and pleasure of participation in a true team game.

In a modern world it is inevitable that a game such as curling should evolve into a sport, with its participants dedicated to the pursuit of excellence. Although this book has deliberately placed its emphasis on curling as a game, it has only done so with the certain knowledge that the game is also the foundation for the sport. But serious competitive curling at national and international level is a further subject with a great many topics to consider, and in time someone will no doubt do it justice.

Curling as a game will need both its supporters and serious investment. Ice rinks and equipment cost a great deal of money and the running of curling's structures and organisations requires serious commitment from many individuals. Without curlers there will be no curling, and without the foundation of the game there will be no sport.

After a struggle over many years for recognition as something more than a pastime, curling is now a fully accepted winter sport at the Olympic Games. It has its own European and World Championships and is fast gaining popularity as a televised sport. A combination of these developments has ensured an upsurge of interest, new investment and a serious approach to its development, especially through the offices of the RCCC. Quite logically they have turned their initial attention to the promotion of the sport amongst children and beginners, along with the development of facilities and equipment.

This progress does not seek to exclude club curling from development. For club curlers and the sport alike there are groups and societies who cater for every age and level, from youth through to the very senior, yet it is still common to see curlers of all ages curling together with total enthusiasm and clear pleasure. This will never change – in fact, it can only improve. The essence of curling at any level is to do your best and enjoy the game, to share, to give all, to succeed as a team and gain from that the lessons that curling can teach.

It must be stressed that all youngsters will gain from curling what they can't gain anywhere else. They will learn discipline, dedication, commitment, teamwork, confidence, belief in each other; they will develop their characters and their bodies, their minds and their attitude to life. They will acquire social skills and manners, respect for all and respect for the traditions which a modern world doesn't always choose to promote. None of these can be taught convincingly at schools without the help of something as well-suited to the problem as curling. In a sense we are all children, and we can all learn from the game of curling.

It is time to go curling. Let us all form a team and delight in the game, playing our stones and sweeping the others. Let us enjoy each other's company and skills and this wonderful game of life which has room for us all. If we do, it will prosper beyond our dreams.

Ice Rinks

The following information is to enable curlers to locate the ice rink most convenient to them. It contains the name of the rink, a short address and contact number, how many sheets of ice it provides and when curling ice is available, the normal nature of the ice, the date of construction and nature of the base under the ice and, where relevant, further comments supplied by the rinks. This is followed by a list of the clubs which are based there.

Scotland

ABERDEEN

Stoneywood Road, Dyce, Aberdeen 01224-724454
6 sheets, Oct - Apr Keen ice 1983 - concrete base

Aberdeen Aberdeen and District Rotary Aberdeen Ladies AWW Aberdeen Gr Sch Former Pupils Aberdeen Petroleum Banchory Bank of Scotland Aberdeen Bon-Accord Donald's Curling Club Clydesdale Bank (Aberdeen) Grampian Construction Huntly Grampian Ladies Granite City Ladies Haddo House Laurencekirk Marischal Meldrum and Daviot Northern Lights Pecten Rubislaw Tarland Turriff Ugie

ATHOLL (Pitlochry)

Lower Oakfield, Pitlochry 01796-473337
4 sheets, Oct - Mar Keen ice 1982 - sand base
Some heaving

Blair Atholl Breadalbane Aberfeldy Breadalbane Academy Breadalbane Kenmore Grantully Heart of the Highlands Kinloch Rannoch Logierait Murthly/Murthly Castle Oakfield North Perthshire Young Curlers Pitlochry Pitlochry High School Pitlochry Ladies Toberargan Tullymet Weem

AVIEMORE

Aviemore Mountain Resort, Aviemore   01479-810624

7 sheets, Sep - Apr   Keen, swingy ice   1966 - concrete base
Ice all year; small heave; planned new facility

Aberlour   Aviemore   Aviemore and District Young Curlers
Badenoch Police   Cairngorm Ladies   Carrbridge   Donavon   Kingussie
Lochaber   Newtonmore   Strathspey

AYR

9 Limekiln Road, Ayr   01292-268000

6 sheets, Sep - Apr   Keen "beautiful" ice   1973 - sand base
Ice all year except July

"40" Curling Club   Auchenames   Auchencruive   Ayr & Alloway
Ayr   Ayr & District Round Table   Ayr Juniors   Ayr Country Club
Ayr Cricket Club   Ayr Rotary   Ayrshire & Arran Health Board
Ayrshire Association of Vets   Ayrshire Cattle Club   Ayrshire Rotary
Ayr Y F C   Bank of Scotland   Beresford Ladies   Between the Sheets
British Legion   Broomley Ladies   Bute   Carnell   Carrick   Cellar
Crosshill   Civil Service Sports Council   Construction League
Crossmichael   Crossroad & District Y F C   Cumnock "41" Club
Culroy   Cumnock & District   Cumnock Rotary   Dailly   Darvel
Dalmellington Craigengillan   Doonfoot   Dundonald   Fairywell
Fullarton   Galston Haymouth   Gangrels   Girvan   Girvan Ladies
Gourock Ladies   Greenock Ladies   Icebergs   Irvine   Irvine Ladies
Kilmarnock Ladies   Kilmarnock Townend   Kilwinning Eglinton
Kirkmichael   Kirkoswald   Kyle & Carrick D.C.   Kylestrome
Lady Margaret Ladies   Largs Thistle   Loudoun Rotary   Mauchline
Mardi Ladies   New Cumnock   Mauchline & District Y F C
Newhouse   Ochiltree   Prestwick St Nicholas G.C.   Riccarton
Probus   Robert Scott   Royal Bank of Scotland   Scottish Rotary
Sanquhar & Upper Nithsdale   Seniors Club   Sorn   St Andrews
Springside/Dreghorn   St Columba Church   St Leonards Ladies
St Leonards (Sunday League)   Stair   Strathclyde Police   Stratton
Symington   Tarbolton   Tarbolton Ladies   Threepwood
Troon Portland   Troon Rotary

BORDER (Kelso)

Abbotseat Road, Kelso 01573-224774

4 sheets, Oct - Mar Slow ice 1964 - concrete base

Ayton Castle Chirnside Coldstream and Hirsel Duns Earlston Foulden Gala Water Glendale Greenlaw Jedburgh Kelso Lammermuir Lauderdale Lees Roxburghe Selkirk Royal Bank of Scotland (Border District) St Boswells St Ronans Swinton Teviotdale Yester

BRORA

Royal Marine Hotel, Golf Road, Brora 01408-621252

4 sheets, Oct - Mar Keen, swingy ice 1984 - concrete base Condensation

Brora Dornoch Halkirk Locheye and St Duthus Rogart Royal Marine Struie Sutherland Juniors

DUMFRIES ICE BOWL

King Street, Dumfries 01387-251300

6 sheets, Sep - Apr Keen, good ice 1992 - concrete base

Caerlaverock Cairn Colvend Crocketford Dalbeatie Dumfries Dumfries Ice Bowl Ass. Lochfoot Loreburn Kirkpatrick-Durham New Abbey Parton Ruthwell Tongland Sanquhar & Upper Nithsdale

EAST KILBRIDE

Olympic Centre, East Kilbride 01355-244065

5 sheets, Oct - Apr Keen ice 1988 - concrete base Condensation at times

Beechnuts Eaglesham East Kilbride Lynn & Clarkston Phoenix Whitecraigs Curling and Sporting Society

ELGIN

Borough Briggs Road, Elgin   01343-541677

5 sheets, Sep - Apr   Keen ice   1993 - ins. concrete base
Low emissary ceiling installed

Allied Distillers Ltd   Ballindalloch   Bank of Scotland (Highland)
Buckie   Darnaway   Dufftown   Elgin   Elgin Rotary Club
Fochabers   Forres   Sunninghill

FOREST HILLS (Aberfoyle)

Trossachs Club, Aberfoyle   01877-387277

4 sheets, Sep - Apr   Slow, swingy ice   1984 - concrete base
New ice plant installed

Balfron   Buchlyvie   Castle   Club 90   Forest Hills Trossachs
Loch Ard   Port of Menteith   Strathendrick   Thornhill

FORFAR

Suttieside Road, Forfar   01307-468668

7 sheets, Oct - Mar   Keen, swingy ice   1988 - concrete base
Ice all year

Aberlemno   Baldovan   Balruddery   Braeknowe   Broughty Ferry
Claverhouse   Cortachy   Dundee   Dundee Ladies   Forfar
Forfar Ladies   Forfar Young Curlers   Forthringham   Glamis
Kirkinch and Nevay   Kirriemuir   Kirriemuir and District Ladies
Lundie and Auchterhouse   Monifieth   Newport   Panmure
Pearsie   Pitkerro   Suttieside   University of Dundee

GALLEON CENTRE

99 Titchfield Street, Kilmarnock   01563-524014

5 sheets, Sep - Apr   Keen ice   1987 - ins. concrete
Ice all year

Clydesdale Cricket Club CC   Galleon   Riccarton

GOGAR PARK

Gogar Station Road, Edinburgh 0131-3391254
4 sheets, Sep - Apr Keen/swingy ice 1979 - concrete base

Athelstaneford Bank of Scotland Boswall Buchan Carrington Currie and Balerno Dominies Dept. of Agriculture and Fisheries Dundas Edinburgh Rotary Gogar Park Gogar Park Young Curlers Haymarket Heriot-Watt Livingston Manse MRC Oatridge Pentlands Tuesday Club Uphall Vat 69 West Linton

GREENACRES

Howwood, Renfrewshire 01505-850633
6 sheets, Sep - Apr Swingy ice 1979 - sand base
Some heaving; continually upgrading

71 Club Alternative Ardgowan Barony Barrhead Fereneze Beith Morishill Beith Morishill Ladies Blythswood Bridge of Weir Brookfield Cardross Dalry Union Drystanes Erskine Gleniffer Greenacres Junior Curling Club Greenacres Ladies Howwood Kilbarchan Kilmacolm Lochwinnoch Minerva Neilston Old Grammarians Paisley St Mirren Reform Sproulstoun Uplawmoor

GREEN HOTEL

2 The Muirs, Kinross 01577-863467
4 sheets, Sep - Apr Keen ice 1977 - sand base

Abercorn Aberdour Bank of Scotland (Fife) Bishopshire Boreland Broomhall Ceres Crawford Priory Dalgety Bay Dollar Academy Dollar and Devon Dale Dunfermline Ladies Dunfermline Fossoway Fossoway Ladies Glenfarg Ladies Glenrothes Inverkeithing Keith Kinross Kinross Junior Kinross Ladies Orwell Orwell Ladies Queich Stratheden Stratheden Ladies Tulliallan

HARVIES (Stevenston)

Saltcoats Road, Stevenston 01294-605126
4 (+ 2 junior) sheets, Sep - April Keen ice 1988 - ins. concrete base Ice all year

Ardrossan Castle Auchenames Between the Sheets Largs Thistle Millport Skelmorlie

INVERNESS

Bught Park, Inverness 01463-235711

5 sheets, Sep - Mar Variable ice 1967 - concrete base
Little insulation

41 Curling Club Alness Ardclach Avoch Beauly Belmaduthy Bught Ladies Caberfeidh Cawdor Citadel Dalcross Fairburn Dept of Agr. and Fisheries, Scotland - Highland Highland Ladies Highland Highlands and Islands Dev. Board Inverness Hospitals Insurance Institute of Inverness Inverness Inverness Teachers Inverness Ice Rink Ladies Killearnan Ledgowan Loch Ness Kingsmills Sea Angling and Sporting Club Muir of Ord Nairn Nairn Ladies Northern Constabulary (Inverness) Ross-shire Ladies Strathpeffer Spa The Fifteen Club Torness

KIRKCALDY

Rosslyn Street, Kirkcaldy 01592-595100

6 sheets, Sep - Mar Variable ice 1938 - concrete base
Due to skating, staff have little time to prepare curling ice.

Aberdour Balcaskie Balwearie High School Staff Boreland Cambo Cambo Ladies Ceres Crawford Priory Cupar Dunfermline Falkland Forret Glenrothes Hercules Ladies Hercules Inverkeithing Kennoway Kirkcaldy Ice Rink Largo Leven Lundin and Montrave Markinch Pitlessie Rothes Raith and Abbotshall Raith and Abbotshall (Ladies) St Andrews Stratheden Ladies Strathkinnes Thornton

LAGOON LEISURE CENTRE

Mill Street, Paisley 0141-8894000

6 sheets, Sep - Apr Keen ice 1992 - concrete base

Bearsden Ski Club Clydesdale Bank (Gl.) Kelvin Old Glenalmond

LANARKSHIRE (Hamilton)

off Muir Street, Hamilton 01698-282448

6 sheets, Sep - Apr Average ice 1967 - base unknown

Alpha Ladies Avondale Heather Bathgate Bellshill Blantyre Bothwell Bothwell Castle Bothwell Ladies Cadzow Calder Cambuslang Cambusnethan Carstairs & District Coulter Dippool Douglas East Kilbride and Haremyres Glasgow and District Rotary Hamilton and Thornyhill Hamilton Ladies Hamilton Ice Sports Club Lanark Lanark Ladies Lanarkshire Young Curlers Lesmahagow Lesmahagow Ladies Section New Monkland Stra'ven Ladies Strathaven Golf Upperward Ladies Wirsels Ladies Wishaw

LETHAM GRANGE

Colliston, by Arbroath 01241-890373

4 sheets, Oct - Mar Keen, swingy ice 1984 - concrete base
Equipment needs renewal

Arbroath Brechin Castle Catterthun Dalhousie Ladies Dun Edzell Evenie Water Fettercairn Fordoun Letham Grange Letham Grange (Ladies' Section) Southesk

LOCHGOILHEAD

Drimsynie Leisure Centre, Lochgoilhead 01301-703247

4 sheets, Nov - Mar Swingy ice 1986 - concrete base

Benmore and Kilmun Cairndow Drimsynie Ladies Dunoon Argyll Dunoon Ladies Inveraray Loch Goil Oban Strachur Tighnabruaich Upper Cowal

MAGNUM

Harbourside, Irvine 01294-278381

7 sheets, Sep - Mar Keen ice 1977 - concrete base
Ice all year; plant problematic

Irvine Kilwinning Eglinton Magnum Skelmorlie Stewarton Heather

MURRAYFIELD (Edinburgh)

Riversdale Crescent, Edinburgh 0131-3467353

6 sheets, Sep - Apr Ins. concrete base

37 Club Abbotsford Curling Society Aberlady Biggar
Boswall Bank of Scotland (Edinburgh) Broughton United Bruce
Bruntsfield Curling Society Chartered Surveyors (Edinburgh)
Clydesdale Bank (Edinburgh) Coates Corstorphine Dalkeith
Corstorphine Ladies Dept. of Agriculture and Fisheries, Scotland
Dirleton Duddingston Dundas & Wilson C.S. East Linton
Eddleston Edinburgh Academicals Edinburgh B.M.A. Ladies
Edinburgh Curling Club Edinburgh Ladies Edinburgh Medical
Ford Ladies George Heriot School George Watson's Haddington
Holyrood Libberton and Quothquan Lothian Health Board Staff
Lothian Ladies Lowland Brigade Merchiston Midcalder
Musselburgh National Coal Board Newlands and Tarthwater
Oxenfoord Peebles Penicuik Pentland Ladies SIAE Super
Stewart's Melville F.P. Temple The Musketeers Watsonian
The Royal Bank of Scotland (Edinburgh District) West Linton

PERTH

Dewar's Rinks, Glover Street, Perth 01738-624188

8 sheets, Sep - Apr Keen, swingy ice 1989 - Ins. concrete base
Ice all year - ice lifted or prepared for special occasions

Abdie Abdie Ladies Abercairney Airleywight Airleywight Ladies
Ardblair Ardoch Auchterarder Ballathie Blackford and Carsebreck
Bank of Scotland (Perth and District) Breadalbane Glendochart
Breadalbane Glenorchy Breadalbane Killin Blairgowrie Clunie
Carse of Gowrie Ladies Clydesdale Bank (Perth) Comrie
Coupar Angus and Kettins Craigie Hill Crieff and Auchtertyre
Delvine Dept. of Agriculture and Fisheries, Scotland (Perthshire)
Drummond Castle Dunkeld Dunkeld Ladies Dunning Dunsinane
Errol Fair City Ladies Findo Gask Fingask Forteviot Glendoick
General Accident Glenfarg Glenshee Kilgraston and Moncreiffe
Kilgraston and Moncrreiffe Ladies Kinfauns Kinnochtry Leuchars
Lynedoch Ladies Meikleour Methven Muirend Muthill Perth
Perth and Kinross Teachers Perth Ladies Perth Royal Infirmary
Perthshire Medical Royal Army Service Corps Memorial Club
Pitheavlis Rattray Rossie Schiehallion Ladies Scone and Perth

St Martins Strathallan Meath Moss Strathmore
The Royal Bank of Scotland (Dundee and Perth District)

SOUTH OF SCOTLAND (Lockerbie)

14 Glasgow Road, Lockerbie 01576-202197
5 sheets, Sep - Apr Keen ice 1967 - ins. concrete base

Annan Annandale Speakers Applegarth and Sibbaldbie Aspatria Auchencairn Balcastle Construction Borgue Buittle Corrie Craigielands Craignair Crossmichael Cummertrees Dalbeattie Dalbeattie and District Ladies Dalton St Bridget's Dryfesdale Dumfries Police Durisdeer Eskdale Gretna and Border Hutton Hollywood Johnstone and District Kelton Kentside Probus Kirkcudbright Country Kirkmahoe Kirkmichael Lochrutton Kirkpatrick Durham Lochmaben Castle Lockerbie Schools Lockerbie Young Curlers Loreburn Morton New Abbey Nithsdale Ladies Parton Penpont Royal Fourtowns Ruthwell SOAEFD Symington (Lanarkshire) Threave Ladies Waterbeck Three Counties Medical Victoria Ladies

STIRLING

Williamfield, Stirling 01786-450389
6 sheets, Sep - Apr Keen ice 1980 - sand base
Planned new concrete floor

Airthrey Castle Argyle & Sutherland Highlanders Balfron Blairdrummond Bonnybridge Borestone and Stirling Buchlyvie Bridge of Allan Callander and Trossachs Campsie Glen Denny Cumbernauld Daytime Men's Club Dollar & Devondale Doune Dollar Ladies Drymen Dunblane Dunblane Thistle Falkirk Falkirk Ice Rink Falkirk Ladies Falkirk Ladies (1960) Fintry Forth Valley Health Board Forth Valley Ladies Grangemouth Keir Kilsyth Kilsyth Ladies Kippen Laurieston and Zetland Larbert Lenzie Ladies Linlithgow Port of Menteith Sauchie and Bannockburn Stirling and District Ladies Stirling Ice Rink Young Curlers Strathendrick Ladies Strathkelvin The '80' Torbrex Tulliallan West Stirlingshire Ladies

STRANRAER

North West Castle Hotel, Stranraer 01776-704413

4 sheets, Oct - Apr Keen ice 1970 - sand base

Anwoth & Girthon Borgue Castle Kennedy Girvan Glasserton
Girvan Ladies Colmonell Grants Kirkcowan Kirkinner
Kirkmabreck Leswalt Limekiln Loch Loch Connel Logan
Minnigaff Mochrum Old Luce Penninghame Portpatrick
Stoneykirk Stranraer Ice Rink Tongland Twynholm Wigtown

SUMMIT CENTRE (Glasgow)

Closed. A new rink will accommodate these clubs in 1999.

69 Alma Bank of Scotland (Glasgow) Bearsden Belmont Ladies
Cadder Carmunnock and Rutherglen Cathcart Castle Crossmyloof
Cawder House Clyde Ladies Druids Dumbarton Duntocher
Dumbreck Ladies Duntocher Ladies Firwood Ladies Giffnock
Glasgow Academicals Glasgow Ladies Glasgow Schools
Glasgow XX Helensburgh Kelvinside Academicals
Kelvinside Academy Maxwell Ladies Nondescripts
October Ladies Partick Pollok Rolling Stones
Royal Bank of Scotland (Glasgow District) The Curlews
Scottish Power Glasgow & Clyde Victoria Ladies (Glasgow)

WATERFRONT LEISURE CENTRE

Customhouse Way, Greenock 01475-797979

4 sheets, Sep-Apr Keen, swingy ice 1997 - concrete base
Ice all year

Ardgowan Ardgowan Barony Bute Druids Gourock
Gourock Ladies Greenock Ladies Newark Port Glasgow

England

Ice rinks that provide curling are few and far between in England, and ice conditions are said to be poor. There are plans for a curling rink near Preston, but for the present English curlers travel abroad for their curling. Those in the North use Lockerbie and Kelso. The English Championships are held annually at a Scottish rink. Further information can be obtained from:

Secretary, ENGLISH CURLING ASSOCIATION

Eric Hinds, Little Wethers, Sandy Lane, Northwood,
Middlesex HA6 3HA
01895-201000

Secretary, ECA Ladies' Branch

Miss S Johnston, 11Whitingford, Edinburgh EH6 5TB
0131-5537618

Although most English clubs are small, they are all listed here.

Bradford Chelmsford Riverside City of London Glendale
Hampstead London Northerners London Watsonians Mogador
Peterborough Preston Richmond Ladies Surrey and Sussex
Thames Wigan & Haigh

Ireland

There are not as yet ice rinks in Ireland that provide curling, but efforts by the Irish Curling Association continue to change the situation. For those of either Irish birth or parentage who wish to join the association please contact their secretary:

John Burns, Rose Cottage, Drygrange, Melrose TD6 9DJ.
01896-849626

There are six Irish clubs who curl at various Scottish rinks:

Ailsa Craig   Atlantic   Bann   Belfast   Clandeboye and Kiltonga
Leinster

Wales

The Welsh Curling Association was founded in 1973. Rinks curl at Deeside and travel regularly to Scotland and Europe for competitions. In the past poor facilities have held back the association's aspirations, but with the new ice rink (opens September 1998) their hopes are high.

New members are welcome and there is a large juniors section. For details please contact their secretary:

Ann Meikle, 27 Holm Lane, Oxton, Birkenhead
Merseyside 0151-6083691

DEESIDE

Deeside Leisure Centre, Queensferry 01244-814725
6 sheets, Oct - Apr   New, unknown ice   1998 - ins. concrete
Ice all year

Alyn Valley 73   Alun Valley 75   Connah's Quay   Deeside
Deeside Mix & Match   Denbigh Whackers   Denbigh Rolling Stones
Kinnerton Bluebells   Kinnerton Vikings   Sealand   Sealand Sliders

The publishers will be grateful to receive any information which curlers feel will benefit future editions of this book. Please contact the publishers directly.

If schools or coaching organisations wish to have posters or booklets made of sections of this book, contact the publishers for more information.

WS Publishers
The Studio
Old Ballikinrain
Balfron
G63 0LL
Scotland

Tel/fax: 01360-441010